I WISH I WAS BILLY COLLINS

BILLY COLLINS

— POEMS —

BY PETE McLAUGHLIN

I WISH I WAS BILLY COLLINS

— POEMS —

BY PETE McLAUGHLIN

WELLSTONE CENTER
in the Redwoods

Wellstone Books
an imprint of the Wellstone Center in the Redwoods
858 Amigo Road
Soquel, CA 95073
www.wellstoneredwoods.org

CONTENTS

EDITOR'S NOTE

By Kyle VanDrimmelen

"Strikes and gutters, ups and downs."

—The Dude

Not a conversation went by between Pete and me that didn't at some point evoke *The Big Lebowski*. Whether it was our discussions on the benefits of nihilism or our mutual longing to exude a more dude-like existence, we both recognized the great truths that the movie contained and treated it like our bible, a sacred text to be referred back to when answers evaded us and guidance was needed.

The first time I met Pete was at an open-mic reading at the Wellstone Center in the Redwoods near Santa Cruz, California. As an intern for Wellstone Books, I was given the assignment of helping "this funny ex-P.E. teacher that doesn't have a computer" transcribe some lines of poetry into digital format. I showed up expecting to see a mustached man, bent out of shape, wearing a decades-old baseball cap.

Instead, there was Pete, a thin, bouncy fellow donning an SJSU sweater with the sleeves rolled up. I approached him and introduced myself, pointed at his sweater and said I was a Spartan myself. He informed me that he never went to school at San Jose State, but someone he knew gave him the sweater and he liked it. His wardrobe was filled with relics like this, most famously a valet jacket he was known to wear on just about any occasion.

The reading began, and we went around the circle sharing what we considered to be writing. Tom, the Vietnam Vet, read a short piece about a dinner he once had where he discovered a parallel between lobsters being yanked from their tank for cooking and his own experiences back in Nam, sitting around camp with his fellow G.I.'s, waiting for a chopper to swoop in and pick up another batch of soldiers for the battle field.

I read a fabled tale about an egotistical real-estate tycoon becoming the President of the United States, and what his first day in office might be like, including an extended visit to the new gold-plated toilet bowl he'd had installed at the White House. This was March of 2016.

Others read from their nascent novels or memoirs or whatever it was they came to Amigo Road to work on. And then it was Pete's turn. Apparently he always went last and, I quickly learned, for good reason. He was an act that couldn't be followed.

His weapon of choice was a notebook with duct tape around the edges that had been cut and taped and cut and taped. Next to him sat Steve, Wellstone Center co-director, who rattled off titles of poems for Pete to read, each one killing harder than the last.

"Angry Prius"

Killed.

"Shopper's Corner"

Murdered.

"I Wish I Was Billy Collins"

Destroyed.

Pete was proud enough of "Shopper's Corner" that he gave a copy of it to one of the "fresh-faced checkers" that inspired it. The young lady enjoyed it so much that she ran off copies and passed them around to *all* her fellow checkers. And all was fine, for a while – until Pete decided to pen a follow-up piece in which he retells the

2

events of a psychotic breakdown he incurred amongst these same "fresh-faced checkers," leading to him being dragged out of Shopper's Corner in a straightjacket.

Surprisingly, the checkers were not as enamored with "How Am I?" as they were with "Shopper's Corner."

Within a few days, Pete received a knock on the door from one of Santa Cruz's finest.

"Is there a Pete or Peter McLaughlin here?"

"Yes."

"Do you write poems?"

"Yes."

"Well, the folks at Shopper's Corner would prefer it if you kept them to yourself."

Over the next month, we met two or three times a week and put the scribbles in his notebook onto a Word document, breaking them up into lines that we both ironically referred to as "poetry." Every now and then, when a joke really hit, and Pete knew it, he would stand up from the table we were "working" at and take a victory lap around the room, two fists raised above his head, stating, "Peter McLaughlin, feast your eyes, published Poet." At other times he would anxiously pace back and forth, convinced that he was a fraud and a thief and that he never had an original thought, contemplating whether or not he should wrap the notebook back up in duct tape, bury it in his closet and go back to his simple life of grabbing brunch at the Buttery in between running marathons and masturbating.

I admit this anxiety was not helped by my leaving messages on his answering machine from "The law offices of Feldstein and Gould, calling to inform you of a class action lawsuit being filed against you on behalf of the creative community."

I told Pete he could end this treachery if he simply picked up the phone. But he was a devoted screener of calls. If you wanted to talk with him, you had to leave a message on his answering machine stating your name and business and wait ten to twenty seconds for him to pick up. Otherwise you would receive a call back at some later time from "No Caller ID," which was code for Pete.

But Pete was a strikes and gutters kind of guy. Whether he was manic-depressive or bipolar, I'm not sure. But I know he could go from killing it at an open mic, getting high off the praise thrown his way via laughs and compliments, to feeling completely worthless an hour later, cursing his existence. I remember, on nights he did particularly well, talking with him outside afterwards, asking what his plans were for the next day.

"Tomorrow?" he said, as if the thought of thinking that far forward was a strain. "Tomorrow… is going to be rough."

It's a shame when a person doesn't know just how valued they are. I can't count how many times Pete made my day. With a little quip here or a word of advice there, he altered my life's path in a significant way. And I know for a fact that I'm not alone in that regard. I believe the measure of a person's life is the size of the hole they leave when their time on earth comes to an end. It can be a massive fissure felt by many or a small crack spanning a few folks. Something tells me Pete's absence is both, whether you were a stranger that passed by him as he played his trumpet at Seacliff, looking out at the surf (he was known to fuel runners with the theme music from *Rocky*) or a fortunate confidant who had the pleasure of knowing him. And to the people that never encountered Pete, they have no idea what they missed out on.

The truth is these poems weren't necessarily meant to be read; they were meant to be performed by the man that wrote them. Much of their brilliance was contained in the subtle shifts in tone, slight pauses, and other delivery techniques employed by Pete when he presented them to his lucky audiences. As the editor of this work, it was my job to work with Pete and break them down into a form that best captured this essence. What you have before you is a transcript of an act put on by my good friend Pete McLaughlin, who I love and miss dearly.

I WISH I WAS BILLY COLLINS

I wish I was Billy Collins.

No, not George Clooney, just good old Billy C.

I bet Billy lives in some

charming upstate hamlet,

probably New York or Vermont.

His house is rustic and inviting

no gate, just a hand-painted peace sign out front

and a box that says "free rhubarb, take some"

a wrap-around porch and swing,

tasteful unpretentious curtains,

a happy chimney whispering out aromatic smoke,

and there's always an apple pie

cooling on the window sill.

And so here I come now—

Yes! It's me, fantasy Billy

smiling the smile of the successful

rolling up in my vintage

(but not gaudy)

'56 Chevrolet pickup

my dog Thoreau, a rescue of course, riding shotgun

manic chickens scattering crazily as I pull in.

You see,

I was in town, at the diner,

with Clem and Lefty and Cecil

sipping coffee and discussing

the high school football team's prospects.

It's fall—everything is beautiful.

My wife, who works with orphans,

has just come in from her pottery studio.

She kisses me and informs me

that my agent called and Harvard

wants to honor me again next month.

"Oh how tiresome," I say.

"I'd rather play horseshoes with Clem."

But I go anyway.

Some wealthy hedge-fund alum

whose literary daughter has all my books

dispatches his pilot to fetch me.

He glides into our cow pasture at the appointed hour.

We don't have cows any more,

too much work.

But it's nice not having to drive to the airport.

I make my speech.

Everyone loves me.

At the reception afterward

as usual

some comely twenty-nine-year-old

grad student

her siren's hand lightly on my lapel

lets me know just how much

my work has meant to her....

but I'm used to this by now

so it's no trouble.

I'm such a great guy.

Back at my hotel suite

I toss off a quick

poem

for the *New Yorker*

and sleep soundly as always.

I even wear pajamas.

My children all work for Oxfam

and are expert mountain climbers.

I never need Viagra

my eyes are 20/20

my teeth so sound

the dentist has me visit

only once a year.

But sometimes...on quiet evenings

when I'm tinkering with the Chevy

(I call her Sylvia, after Sylvia Plath)

the Red Sox game quietly on the radio

I find myself wishing I lived in Santa Cruz…yes

in a musty studio apartment

with a decrepit cat who barfs violently on the carpet at four a.m.

it's as though he's trying to turn himself inside out for Christ's sake

and neighbors whose high decibel, jack-hammer style love-making

comes and comes again hard through the cheap-ass half-inch sheet-rock wall

penetrating even the protective pillow I press to my beleaguered ears

and a voodoo smoke alarm with a freaking mind of its own

and a malevolent marauding murder of hoodlum crows

who seem to derive particular glee from shitting only on my car…

But that lasts about two seconds, tops

I shake my head, smiling sheepishly,

and I chuckle softly to my silly Billy self

switch off the light

and head upstairs to bed

to my extraordinary wife

and sleep like a fucking baby.

ANGRY PRIUS

God, do I want to go in the fast lane. Boy oh boy.

Look at them over there,

blithely zooming well over the limit, 75, 80, 85

—just booming down the blacktop like a rolling stampede of high-octane buffalo.

Why, that arrogant golden Hummer was doing 90 just a minute ago,

shimmering wasteful little droplets cascading recklessly from his gleaming dual exhaust.

Does this light-footed asshole in the Birkenstocks know I can do 80, no problem?

Does he know my radio actually gets stations other than NPR?

If I have to listen to Noam Chomsky laconically pontificate

in that superior nasally drone one more goddamn time,

I'll blow a gasket, literally.

Oh, man,

just to chug down gallon after imperialistic gallon one profligate time.

A tank like a reservoir—no guilt, just, "Fill'er up, Daddy-O"

—40 gallons worth, and top that baby off—

let some of that juice just splash right there on the ground.

Oh, to mindlessly drive through the Jack In The Box

blaring Rush Limbaugh or sports talk radio.

To pick up a 12-pack, a Slurpee and a few Lotto tickets at 7-Eleven—

no, make that a case of Keystone Light, a couple tins of Kodiak and a copy of *Hustler*.

And a nasty hot dog too, for the road.

I wonder what it's like to sit in the parking lot of a bar—

not a bistro, a real honky-tonk roadhouse—

a dirt lot, with railroad ties, broken glass,

a stray used condom brazenly lurking on the ground.

Surrounded by battered pick ups and one-eyed Camaros—

malevolent unregistered Harleys,

your red-eyed, blue collar driver

stumbling a bit as he pats around for his keys,

lighting up yet another filterless Camel

as he unlocks your dusty door.

Cruising the back roads to avoid the Smokeys,

weaving boozily into the oncoming lane.

Now he's puking out the window,

then pulling over onto the shoulder to sleep off the spins.

Man, that's what I call living!

But here I am, turtling off to yoga class again—

23 soul-crushing miles an hour.

Go ahead, merge in front of me.

I'm a pussy, it's obvious.

Don't worry, I won't honk.

Everybody knows it. Priuses are freaking mute.

Oh please peel these pewling sanctimonious bumper stickers

off my oh so progressive ass.

Obama, Dalai Lama, celebrate diversity, PBS rainbow bullshit.

I want mudflaps!

Yosemite Sam—Back off motherfucker!

Or maybe even those sexy metallic bombshell silhouettes.

I want to tow twin jet-skis to a lake full of white trash.

I want horny, just-acquainted people to screw vigorously inside me

and in a semi-public place, too!

Buddy, if this little blue Prius is a-rockin',

don't come around a-knockin', y'hear?

Shakespeare festival, men's group, health food store, farmers' market,

all the other pious hybrids with their carpool stickers,

some with those smarmy, self-important vanity plates:

SIPS GAS, GRN-CAR, 50 MPG.

Hey, here's an idea—

let's just go first the next time we get to the intersection

at the same time as another car.

Always patronizingly waving everybody through—

"You. No, you. No, after you, please, I insist."

Would somebody just fucking go already!

Christ, it's like Mr. Rogers Neighborhood 24-7 when you're a Prius.

I mean, could there somehow be Prozac

in the gas this bozo's been feeding me?

I know he gobbles that stuff like it's flippin' candy.

Can you imagine Steve McQueen driving me? Sean Connery? John Wayne?

The Duke in a Prius.

The ultimate American icon hunched forward,

sipping chai and listening to Terry Gross,

chatting on a Bluetooth. Come on.

But so today it looks like we're off to pick up the kid at Montessori,

drop him off at the cello lesson, then to the tutor's.

Poor cosseted little sap, slathered in sunscreen whenever he leaves the house,

kale smoothies, vegan sushi, kombucha, children's mindfulness group on Saturdays.

Good Lord, he even does Sudoku already.

He'll certainly never drive a Bronco, an F-150, or a 4x4 Jeep

with those awe-inspiring monster-truck tires.

Unmufflered engine gurgling and growling like an apex predator.

Towering, no, lording above the traffic,

maybe even a roll bar, fog lights—the whole works, why not?

And a fine young honey—

in cutoffs and halter of course,

snuggled right up close,

reeking of hairspray and wine coolers,

deftly making him feel every inch a real man,

if you know what I mean…

Belligerently blasting through the yellow as it turns red,

Old Glory waving unapologetically from the roll bar.

Mercilessly tailgating all comers,

even senior citizens, the handicapped.

Relentlessly changing lanes without signaling—

swerving provocatively in and out.

You got a *problem* with that?

Going off-road, 4-wheel drive, baby.

Bouncing and shaking like it's an earthquake,

the hairspray girl rapturously squealing,

one of those winches with a cable on the front,

in case your bro gets in a jam.

Oh my God—

I just thought of it: a gun rack—

the Holy Grail,

the ultimate phallic vehicular accessory—

a freaking gun rack…

Oh, I need one, I so do.

Listen, I'll drive in the slow lane forever—

"Baby on Board" sign if you want.

Carefully shuttle all those dorky Montessori kids

to tai chi, chess club, kite-flying, whatever.

Re-upholster me with hemp for God's sake if you want.

Hell, slap a "Feel the Bern" sticker on me.

It's all good.

Just let me be the only little bad-ass Prius in the world,

man enough to proudly tote an automatic weapon if need be.

You know, for when the oil does actually dry up,

and it's every thirsty Mad-Max hybrid for himself.

And please let me taste the fast lane once,

just once,

for like 5 glorious full-throttle minutes…

Aggressively flashing my high-beams

at some clueless, Lexus-driving realtor yapping on her cellphone,

honking in repetitive denigrating blasts

at a tentative minivan loaded with three generations of wide-eyed Pakistanis.

C'mon,

let's maniacally flip off a dawdling astigmatic rabbi

in a shit-brown Yaris.

Oh, let me live a little,

just a little,

before the inevitable day when you trade me in,

like a once-scintillating wife you've slowly grown tired of,

on that fully gelded, sexless, lifeless,

smug-as-a-church-lady, no-gas-tank, phone-booth-sized,

ultimate P.C. status symbol,

the electric car.

MIDDLE AGE

I lower myself stiffly onto the toilet.
I wheeze like an out of tune accordion.
I bend over to tie my shoe
a faint girlish moan
slips unbidden from my lips.
There is velcro in my future, I can see.
Tweezers have lately assumed a position of prominence
in my overmatched grooming arsenal.
Bristling rogue hairs
somehow misplaced from a Turkish blacksmith
charge out insolently from my astonished nostrils
congregate seemingly overnight
in defiant gangs about my wax-clogged ears
sprout forth tauntingly at crazed angles
from the chaotic thicket that is my eyebrows...
These mere pikers dwarfed however
by the frightful ursine loners
some over two inches when standing fully upright
that increasingly populate my back and shoulders.
To women under forty, I know
I am a polyp, a traffic cone, road kill
a smiling hapless turd to be nimbly avoided.
My penis no longer takes my ever more urgent calls.

I can't even get past his secretary anymore.
Well mannered twenty-somethings,
lately even those in their early thirties,
hold the door, call me "sir"
"after you sir," their helpful hand
gently on my back.
Oh, I could kill them.
The DMV guy stares at me blankly
with that crushing civil-service poker face
asks simply, "are you sure about that?"
when I list my hair color as brown.
He shrugs obliquely, looks away
when I ask just what he means.
On the rare nights I do get out,
festive women in their sixties and seventies
emboldened by a second glass of merlot
their heavily made-up faces
smiling wildly like The Joker himself
gently run their age-spotted fingertips
along my shoulders, my chest
their overdone eyes seductively narrowed
"mmm" they purr lasciviously
"How do you stay so fit?"
Has it come to this?!
AARP continually beseeches me
to join their incontinent ranks.

No, I'll not do water aerobics

in a urine-filled pool.

I'll not lawn bowl, birdwatch, swing dance,

sing in the disturbingly peppy chorus of Guys and Dolls.

I'll not drive the hour to Shoreline Amphitheater

for the dubious privilege of hearing James Taylor

probably wearing a precautionary diaper himself by now

waveringly croon "Fire and Rain"

for the eight thousandth tear-jerking time

venerated by wistfully grinning Boomers

all singing nostalgically along

their Bics held high

swaying in clumsy arrhythmic unison

a giant Cialis commercial come to life.

No, I won't.

Not unless one of those sixtyish panthers,

hungry for love or something like it

picks up the ticket and a fine French dinner beforehand

plays teasing, exploratory footsie beneath the tablecloth

her unblinking green-light eyes

locked mercilessly onto mine.

She winks knowingly, her big toe somehow in my pocket now

longingly bites her plumped up lower lip.

Oh, I never had a chance.

Playfully she spanks me as I slide into bed

calls me Tiger…yes Tiger

milks me for everything and more
treats me real nice and respectful afterward.
"Do you take cream?"
she sings brightly down the hallway
of her four-bedroom empty nest
as I struggle blearily into my pants.
Yes, it has come to this,
and that's just fine with me.

THE WOMAN OF MY DREAMS

Bedazzler: A device used to affix rhinestones to denim
(generally advertised on late night TV.)

She has no idea what kale is.

Never heard of it.

Chard is a sharp piece of glass.

Syrah a common enough woman's name.

She wears three nicotine patches at a time,

chomps and snaps her way through a case of Big Red a week,

and is only two weeks shy of her six-month chip.

She is impressed by my Red Lobster call-ahead card,

and enjoys amusement parks with no apparent sense of irony.

Her spelling is atrocious, routinely employs apostrophes to denote plurals

- often uses the word "classy" - as in, "that Celine Dion is one classy lady."

My knowledge not only of the names of the pieces on a chessboard,

but indeed the different ways in which they are allowed to move

left her breathless with admiration.

But she can pee pretty much anywhere,

change her own oil,

flirt her way out of a traffic ticket,

and once even had a non-speaking role in a Cinemax late-nite feature

about promiscuous young gym bunnies called "Dumbelles."

Her ride is pure American Muscle

- A jacked up lime-green El Camino

  that gets eight miles to the gallon with mag wheels,

  doors that only open from the outside,

  a smoking muffler precariously wired to the chassis,

  and a profanely defiant NRA bumper sticker

- left to her by her dear departed Shane Sr. —

  a correctional officer on unpaid leave

  due to repeated positive Oxycontin tests

  who suffered a massive coronary after being pepper-sprayed

  during a parent-teacher conference gone horribly wrong.

  (Shane Jr. having sharpied swastikas

  onto the pencil-thin arms of his callow,

  unknowing seventh grade Aryan militia recruits)

  She doesn't like to look back. Tells me,

"What happened in the Grotto, stays in the Grotto,"

  but that Hef was, you guessed it, "a gentleman, real classy."

  O.J. seemed like a decent enough guy

  (really liked the blondes),

  and she once broke Erik Estrada's heart so badly

  she had to take out a temporary restraining order.

  This woman, Wanda is, of course, her name,

  elaborately gilds her curve-hugging,

  slightly peek-a-boo denim cowgirl

  outfits with a Bedazzler

  (unicorns and angels recurrent motifs),

  and selects her lotto numbers

22

by way of an indecipherably complex system
involving astrology, numerology,
her menstrual cycle, and a Ouija board.
Her trailer is immaculate, although the literally hundreds
of frog-themed figurines can be a trifle unsettling
(frog astronauts, frog bodybuilders, frog disco dancers).
The same can be said for her phlegmatic six-foot reticulated python,
Ron Jeremy - to whom I am required to feed weekly live mice,
which disgusts and appalls.
But I have no choice if I am to be allowed to inertly play
"English Patient" to her tender yet insatiable "Naughty Nurse."
(She maintains preferred buyer status with Frederick's of Hollywood.)

To the graveyard-shift Philippine janitors and orderlies
to whom she deals early morning blackjack, she is a goddess:
a big-haired, high heeled, false eyelash batting American Dream.
Just a twinkle of inlaid gold flashes in her fetchingly gap-toothed smile
as she teasingly, demurely leans forward, almost contritely
hauls in the hard-earned chips of yet another befuddled player,
addled as they all are by lack of sleep
and all that creamy jiggling promised-land cleavage,
so close a gambling-addicted, pidgin-speaking father of six
could almost reach out and touch it. Paradise.
She moonlights ten hours a week cooking the books
for her brother-in-law's paving company,
and when suggestive comments are good-naturedly broached

by the grimy asphalt-slingers
as they clomp in to pick up their week's wages
— randy verbiage that could quite legitimately be construed
by any emancipated Ensler-reader as sexual harassment—
Wanda merely giggles and takes it as a compliment.
"You wish" or "In your dreams, cowboy," she might shoot back
with a haughty toss of her platinum curly-cue extensions
— teetering endearingly as she minces to the bleeping microwave
in her five-inch faux Jimmy Choos, tugging girlishly at the hem
of her pink leather mini-skirt (Frederick's of course)
to retrieve her steaming pizza-pocket lunch,
Diet Dr. Pepper Big Gulp half-drained on the desk,
by now flavorless Big Red daintily spit into a Post-It
and dropped by accident into the paper shredder.

My push-up princess had a tramp stamp
back when it actually meant something
(Thank God I don't know exactly what.
But in my mind's eye all I can see is bikers, pool tables,
and free clinic penicillin shots).
A winsome butterfly that can occasionally be glimpsed
fluttering skyward from out of her modest middle-aged muffin top
as she reaches up to dust that highest shelf
reserved exclusively for Kermit and Miss Piggy.
What is it I see in this uncultured hussy
—to whom salad means iceberg drenched with lite bacon ranch,

"Dr. Quinn, Medicine Woman," engrossing high drama?

Well, say you were to take the best, and hopefully some of the worst,

of Angie Dickinson, Jessica Hahn, Sarah Palin, Charo and Vanna White

—mixed it all together and threw in just a pinch of Anna Nicole Smith.

This is where you'd alchemically arrive—Wanda.

My one and only Wanda

—who knows exactly what it takes

(along with her recently paroled half-sister, Shonda)

to motivate an otherwise mild-mannered, graying Billy Collins wannabe

to clamber inside a dank, ammonia-smelling second-hand frog costume

and hop frantically about an off-kilter double-wide

croaking to beat the band.

Oh yes, Wanda does know things.

Things I hadn't ever had the temerity to even imagine. . . .

ice cubes, tuning forks, lederhosen. . .

And to think that if that humdrum day at the Goodwill

I hadn't, for some mysterious reason, kismet it must be called,

paused to pick up off the shelf

a tiny porcelain amphibian dressed as a matador,

silently wondering, "Who on earth buys this shit?"

I'd probably be stuck right now

eating kale and drinking Syrah

with one more repressed Match.com striver

who wouldn't know a Bedazzler

if it bit her in the ass.

SHOPPER'S CORNER

They sense me when I enter
alert, at their registers
I always go left
toward the freezer section
but their eyes burn
their searing molten
desire
into my muscular back
as I stride toward the cheese
"He's here" they titter
to one another
like exotic birds — chirping and singing
in some well tended aviary
blondes, brunettes, redheads...
The Shopper's checkers
recognize quality when they see it
in a self-assured
middle-aged man
who knows his way around
the produce section.

Oh how they yearn
to scan my purchases

demurely, coquettishly
they ask
"How are you today?"
"Fine, just fine"
I say
"Would you like a bag today?"
they query suggestively
"No, thank you" I say
the tension palpable
as she counts out the change
drops it into
the strong patient palm
of my waiting hand
her fingertips gently
graze mine
her limpid eyes
unafraid.

I know she desires
to tell me everything
but the line
at checkstand four
cares not a whit
the moment passes
I step out into the unfriendly din
of Soquel Ave.

Perhaps she has a dog

talks to the beast

about the unassuming

salt and pepper haired man

modest and kind

"Why can't the boys my age..."

her voice trails off

"Oh what's the use?" she cries

flinging herself onto the bed

"I love him so!"

HOW AM *I*?

Oh doctor, she had no idea,

let me tell you

I crowed or perhaps even cackled,

the strait jacket's benign embrace

a relief after a half century

of fruitless flailing

existential, romantic, professional.

Hah! The inane spasticity of the hopeful

mercifully shackled at last.

But how could she have known, the innocent lamb?

This dull-eyed beauty school-bound nymphet

artlessly bagging my meager bachelor's provisions.

Why the bananas on the bottom? The beans above?!

The yogurt forlornly on its side,

miserably lactating onto the heedless granola,

dripping downward,

weakening the bag's bottom

the contents ultimately spilling through

onto the all too grimy sidewalk.

Where was I?

Ah, yes—but first a cigarette.

(I don't actually smoke, but I so enjoy

watching Herr Dismal Doktor fumble with the pack,

and like a new lover, tenderly insert

the cancerous cylinder between my lascivious lips,

inexpertly incandescing the horrid little torch…)

Oh, I see I've done it again, excuse me.

Her mistake? Her unwitting conversational blunder?

Simply bad timing, really.

The luck of the draw, as they say.

"How are you today?" her catalytic utterance.

Perversely akin to those fictional scenes

in which a supposedly unaware shopper

is subsumed in an avalanche of streamers and confetti

for the happy accident

of being the millionth catatonic cart-pusher

this feather-light "How are you today?" — innocuous, perfunctory,

the simplest wisp of verbiage, a mere electron if you will—

broke this hapless, humpless camel's metaphysical back,

collapsed a crumbling psychic levee,

uncaged horrible hibernating hounds

of alienation and despair.

Oh doctor! The look of abject horror

on her rather formless features.

A great white shark, I leapt for her!!

Seized her milky innocent shoulders!

Showering her with spittle.

Yes, hah, spiteful spittle indeed.

HOW AM I!? HOW AM I, YOU ASK!?

Oh, the exquisite rapture of sudden, unanticipated release.

The mortified establishment fell deathly silent

as my solipsistic soliloquy erupted.

"Well, I'm constipated because all I eat is cereal and cheese sandwiches,

with a compulsory carrot here and there.

I consume copious handfuls of raisins, but I haven't shit

for three days now,

you insensitive harlot.

I've been fighting a losing battle with plantar fasciitis

since the age of nineteen,

my penis is even more depressed than I.

He just lays there and croaks "Why bother?"

the scoundrel.

My skin is extensively sun-damaged,

and that's cumulative you know,

I can't hear conversations at parties

because I never wore earplugs when I jack-hammered,

there's something swimming in my eye that looks a lot like snot.

My noisily nocturnal pussy,

who is well into life number nine,

now consumes only hypo-allergenic tinned food

made exclusively from rabbits at two-fifty a can.

Believe me, I'm not clever enough to make this up!

He drinks bottled spring water and I squirt steroids

into his convulsing maw with a needleless syringe,

and half the time he bites me for my troubles.

My last girlfriend became a lesbian after we broke up,

I haven't been out of state in eight years,

during my last breakdown my mother called my ex-wife

who called my old best friend

and his wife thinks somehow they should find a way

to sneak crushed-up medication into my food.

In other words, now everybody knows I'm crazy!!"

I released the shaken strumpet

and she ran smack into the automated glass door,

sliding down into a motionless whimpering heap.

Oh doctor, everyone in the store was rapt,

nobody moved.

They could see I was finished,

as I studiously rearranged the contents

of my brown paper bag.

I've no doubt they were all gratefully counting their dubious blessings;

"There but for the grace of God," and all that you know.

So my raucous rant,

in that sense, had become a charitable act! Ho, Ho!

Sobbing, I was subdued by a well-muscled

and unnecessarily condescending butcher.

"There, there" he cooed into my crimson ear

"It's going to be all right,"

his full nelson as tender as any lover's post-coital clasp.

Serenely I rode the gurney

into the ambulance's antiseptic interior,

the doors slamming solidly shut,

the siren strangely comforting.

I knew then the struggle was over.

Now, if I could only convince

the asinine attendants

in this infernal institution

to not make up the beds so unnervingly tightly…

Ah, but we'll save that for another time,

won't we, my good doctor?

THE ROAD NOT TAKEN

I came to a fork in the road and,

overwhelmed by the existential pressure of the decision,

I turned around and headed home.

And that, my friends, has made all the difference.

I'll never know what lay down that deeply beckoning rutted fork,

but I'm pretty sure it would involve

many unforeseen financial obligations,

hidden risks that the guidebooks don't even begin to convey,

all sorts of complex and involved logistics

and quite possibly even bribes and kickbacks,

so just go ahead and count me right out.

I know I'd forget the sunscreen.

I hate that shit anyway

rubbing all sorts of unpronounceable chemicals all over the place—

then you eat your sandwich,

but you forgot the napkins,

so now you're licking your fingers,

but the sunscreen is still on your hands,

so now you're eating all those chemicals,

can a polyp be far behind?

I think I'll just stay inside.

Does one bring an ATM card down this less beaten path?

Travellers' checks?

Could there be identity theft around the next bend?

Pickpockets?

In Rome one time,

this little Gypsy girl

managed to unzip my faggy little fanny-pack

while her toothless, four-foot high great-grandmother accosted me

(Why do they all wear those heavy black shoes? Is there a Gypsy cat-alogue? An outlet store perhaps in suburban Bucharest, with a gaggle of wild-eyed Gypsy hags gleefully looting everything in sight, like that terrifying scene at the end of *Zorba the Greek?*)

Ahem, accosted me, as I say,

with a vast tattered map,

shouting some sort of gibberish,

aggressively shaking the map in my dumbass tourist face

while the grimy sprite crept underneath the outstretched map,

her grubby little hands expertly rifling my pouch.

She could have castrated me for Christ's sake!

There goes your passport, ATM card—everything!

Where's the consulate?! What are their hours?! Are we insured for this?!

Do I stop my mail while I'm sauntering down this precious affected road?

They'll only hold it three weeks, then what?

Allow some "friend" to pick it up every few days?

Which will probably become once a week.

There are documents with sensitive personal information in there!

Not on your life!

Oh, these road-seekers, they think they're better than you and I

simply because they purchased a one-way ticket to Peru or Mozambique.

Listen, pal, take your *Outside* magazine, your eco-tourism,

your Swiss Army knife and that ridiculous Peruvian hat

and shove it all where the customs agents prefer not to look!

I don't want to hear it,

you goddam pan-flute, steel-drum, didgeridoo-playing poseur!

Dammit! Why do chicks always go for that obvious, clichéd Jack
Johnson bullshit!

Who'll feed the cat?!

He requires very pricey, vet-prescribed food,

orally administered medication every morning without fail,

the correct dosage mind you.

This stuff is not cheap.

Do I start a line of credit at the vet's? Leave a wad of cash--

we're talking hundreds here—

to some Angie's list cat-sitter?

I mean, who becomes a fucking cat-sitter anyway?

Can I drug-test this loser? Background check? Who has the time?!

Oh yeah. Mozambique, right.

Do you know how many vaccinations you need?

Typhoid, malaria, smallpox, TB, lockjaw, Legionnaire's disease, Lyme
disease, mad cow, SARS, West Nile virus—ooh, that's a good one, West
Nile…E. coli, rabies, cholera, jaundice, flesh-eating bacteria?!

Do you really want to risk helplessly witnessing

your own high speed epidermal evisceration

just so you can come home and go to parties

and brag about how great you are

just because you saw some hippos

and drank fermented monkey spleen

with some guy whose junk is covered up by a paddle

and his four wives all have tits down to their knees

and he spit in your face five times

to supposedly ward off evil spirits?

Oh, he's probably laughing it up with his buddies right now,

"Yeah, I dropped a big-ass loogey

right in that Mzungu's soulless post-colonial devil eyes.

Then I sold him a bracelet

my kid made in school for forty-five dollars.

How is it those imbeciles run the world, anyway?

By the way,

if you trust the FDA with regard to those vaccine ingredients,

you deserve all those cognitive impairments

you're gonna get twenty-five years down the road.

Can you say mercury? aluminum? formaldehyde?

Neurotoxins all.

Just go on the internet, you'll see.

Why don't you just huff a little spray paint

out of a paper bag in the alley.

There's your road less traveled.

It's right behind the 7-Eleven in the bushes by the dumpster.

You don't hear immigrants from those adventure countries

braying about the road less traveled.

You know what they want?

Rental property, Roth IRAs, and a timeshare in Reno.

Listen,

I got the Travel Channel, Discovery, and National Geographic at the library.

There's a pretty good zoo up in San Francisco,

and if I get desperate

there's always Burning Man.

No, scratch that.

I'd rather get dengue fever and be discovered dead

with giant African maggots feasting on my eyeballs

than find myself

taking a freaking selfie at Burning Man.

But if you decide to go, bring plenty of sunscreen.

And probably some condoms too.

See you when you get back.

MAXINE

Two polyester guys
a glass coffee table
shag carpet
2:30 a.m.
You get the picture.
"You want a line, my man?"
Her friends, not mine
they had buzzed us up
last call having puked the dregs
of a Fillmore Street yuppie bar
into further ill-considered pursuits.
"My friends live around the corner"
she had purred.
"Oh, here we go" I had thought.
But now it felt wrong, seedy,
my new lady friend out cold
sideways on the sofa
my new pals
chopping and snorting.
Sensibly, I began my goodbyes
"No thank you. No, no, I'm sure. Nice meeting you though."
But now a burning sensation

my right thigh....stinging somehow

the realization, absurd, comical, horrifying

Good God!

She's peeing on me!

A hot forceful stream

of boozy urine

that final shot—pilfered

from a ham-faced blowhard,

the certain coup de grace,

her equipment now aimed

precisely in my direction

no protecting panties

beneath her Frederick's of Hollywood

black spandex mini dress.

I took it like a man.

Hours prior,

a turgid office party

she a secretary

let go that very day

pouty, petulant, drinking willfully.

Twenty-two and constructed expressly

to eviscerate a man's good sense

"don't even think about it" I thought

(thinking hard)

she's all vixen, big game

you're marshmallow fluff.

But here she came,

stridently, purposefully, almost angrily

a "What the hell, it's a slow night" look

in her blue mascaraed eyes.

Like a grateful puppy

plucked from a humane society basket,

I was pulled to the dance floor

touched inappropriately

and that, as they say,

was that.

The boys in the band looked on, smiling,

nodding approvingly

as she whispered my

suddenly x-rated future

steamy into my ear.

That boy doesn't know what he's in for

the clear consensus.

I called her a week after.

"You know you peed on me, right?"

We came together at the Albion

a Mission district dive

the too-cool hipsters

suspiciously eyeballing us

a square and Pretty Woman

getting loaded in the corner.

She danced for me later

wobbling on high rise stilettos

like a newborn deer

collapsing

in an inebriated heap.

I loved it.

She belittled me

when I brought up condoms

grabbed an economy-size box

flung handfuls in my face.

"Here, you asshole, here are your fucking condoms!"

Apparently she went through

quite a few,

or maybe just bought in bulk.

When I awoke

she had already commenced

rousing me for round two

"I will marry this woman"

I thought.

"Do you wanna get high?" she cooed

"No, no, this is fine" I said.

That was twenty years ago.

I woke last night

To the sounds of my girlish neighbors'

ardent love-making.

Passionately she cried

then all was quiet.

I sighed, smiling wistfully in my aloneness

thinking of women I had known

but thinking most of all

of my exquisite Maxine.

DMV THOUGHTS

Failing stretch pants and wallets on chains

excessive cologne mixing with faint traces of baby powder

molting pre-millennium wigs and condiment-stained wife-beaters

tsunamic comb-overs and precarious dandruffy pompadours

curlers in a church-lady's thinning coiffure

creeping neck tattoos and a 1987 time-warp all polyester employee dress code.

An actual Hooter's t-shirt—on a pregnant young woman no less.

Florescent light and recycled air…a broken dribbling drinking fountain.

Do I look like these people?

Could I somehow be one of them?

Can I maybe get scabies from these seats?

Is that B.O. me?

Hey, don't cut the line lady. I see you.

No way you have an appointment.

Don't let her in—fuck, what are you doing?

Ah, let it go, it's not worth…

Would you shut that toddler up, please!

That's such a fake cry.

It's obvious the kid's flat whining

just give it the goddamn cell phone, all right?

I swear Latino babies are louder than white ones.

Is that racist?

Please don't sit next to me. Please don't sit next to me. Shit.

This guy has weird scabs on his arms,

I can see his ass crack when he leans forward

and of course he wants to talk.

Where are his teeth?!

Why do I always wait 'til the last minute?

Every year. Every fucking year.

That smog guy ripped me off.

A new harmonic balancer—what the hell is that?

Sounds like something you'd get at a store that sells crystals, Yanni CDs.

But I know nothing about cars, nothing.

Real men know about cars—have jobs…

Ooh, that girl getting her license is pretty hot.

Man, those tights they all wear…

God, you fucking pervert!

You're older than her mom—who actually isn't too shabby either.

I wonder what it'd be like to be with both of them.

Dude, you are going to hell. You have no life, none.

Just don't go to any college reunions, okay?

Sitting at the DMV, number B86, when they're only on B68

with Mr. Halitosis picking at his nasty arms

while you have pathetic statutory rape fantasies.

No wonder you're alone.

I wish I was handicapped, they all go right to the front.

Jesus! I hate myself. I really hate myself. What a fucking douchebag.

Man, I have to pee.

But no way I'm using the DMV bathroom,

just hold it—like on that bus in Mexico that time.

It's funny, you can always hold it a lot longer than you think.

But I sure do have to pee a lot these days.

I hope there's nothing wrong with my prostrate.

And why is this skin around my nostrils so dry and flaky lately?

What is this strange new bump on my skull?

But look, I can do all of the eye charts no problem,

and I think that mom just checked me out—I don't see any ring...

Maybe the daughter could just watch us and masturbate,

that's not sex—not technically I think,

maybe a misdemeanor—community service or something...

Coaching kids maybe?

Would You Shut That Baby Up!!

Man, I'm hungry.

Maybe I could walk over to Whole Foods and just get something.

Whole Foods people do all this DMV shit online.

It's so smug in there.

I always feel out of place at Whole Foods—

feel like apologizing or something.

Nine dollars for a turkey sandwich

and no, I don't want to donate my change to the Polar Bear Fund.

Fucking millennial checkers making me feel bad.

Nice haircut, asshole

and when did "no problem" replace "You're welcome"?

Millennials don't even hustle when they jay-walk

they go diagonally and they just freaking saunter.

Give a look, even…

Maybe I could just cruise over and pee in Whole Foods.

That's a much safer bathroom.

Yeah, that's a good idea.

Maybe get some pasta salad, eat it right there, at those nice tables.

They even have free purified water—It's actually pretty sweet in there.

But what if I miss my number? What then?!

What am I even doing here in the first place?

Shit, where's my paperwork?

Did I leave it at home? Did that sketchy doo-rag guy steal it?

Oh, here it is. Jeez, relax…

Man, I really have to go.

BREAKFAST TIME IN APARTMENT #2

Wake and step into shoes naked

(chronically fallen arches explode with ripping

searing pain if this practice not followed

with abstemious rigor of OCD-afflicted

fundamentalist Muslim cleric).

Zombie stagger toward kitchen

with horizontally tumescent member

pointing the way

as a sort of caffeine-seeking dowsing rod.

Bang shin solidly on inert low table as per usual.

Blindly feel for Joe DiMaggio/Mr. Coffee

mini one person size coffee maker

with filter and coffee already

having been introduced during previous

ennui-enshrouded evening passed lugubriously

sulking to Lou Reed monotone nihilism alone in the dark.

Press button and shuffle sleepily to bathroom.

Urinate on floor on both sides of toilet simultaneously,

as penile opening has somehow become clogged,

most likely due to recurring dream of

watching porn at stranger's house,

frustratedly puzzling with

the scrambled Playboy channel

and being emphatically busted

by my middle-school Spanish teacher.

"Ai, Pedro!" she screams, slapping me hard.

"Oh, gracias, Señorita Marshall, muchas gracias,"

I stammer, thrilled by the overt red-handed guilt of it all.

Move to mop up urine with copious ineffective toilet paper.

Note: Rite-Aid toilet paper sucks, as it is thin

beyond any reasonable excrement-absorbing capacity,

even when folded multiple times.

(Resolve to purchase only Trader Joe's brand from now forward.)

Bang head on TP roller,

partially dislodging entire apparatus from wall.

Resign self to future

non-refund of security deposit due to eight years

of similar unreported mishaps.

Don same irregular floodish Dockers as last three days

with gamey running shorts as underwear—also last three days.

Retrieve crusty socks from heaping, chaotic laundry basket.

Shamble back for coffee. Shit, forgot to put water in last night.

Pour in water and jump quickly away as water explodes volcanically

because heating element already at maximum temperature.

Grab broom and sweep up dry cat food broadcast

and subsequently trampled during spastic jump-away maneuver.

Take a minute, smile ruefully, chuckle to self knowingly,

like "ha, ha isn't life funny" when you damn well know

it isn't fucking funny at all.

Tell self it's all a process, recite serenity prayer,

one day at a time, blah blah blah.

Cat is hungry. Sigh heavily, but accept abiding love for cat.

Yes, ex-wife's goddamn cat.

Fleetingly regret chivalrous decision to forego alimony.

Begin drinking coffee. Remove Post-its from kitchen table drawer.

Scrawl self-directed messages such as: "No more excuses!" "You can do it!"

"Why not you!" and affix to kitchen wall.

Feel increasing confidence as caffeine enters bloodstream.

Behave in a Tom-Cruise-like manner;

energetically shadow-boxing and making whooping noises.

Pace back and forth shouting "That's what I'm talkin' 'bout!"

for no apparent reason.

Add in spastic kung-fu chops and kicks where appropriate.

Scoop out cat box and marvel at turd size for seven-pound cat.

Estimate human equivalent to be two to three Presto Logs.

Reflect for a brief sane moment on continued long-term

fruitless adherence to inane Post-it platitudes

garnered from self-help books found at local library.

Declare aloud sarcastically "You got a better idea?"

Take a moment to acknowledge this all has to somehow be your parents' fault.

Derive no comfort. Seethe.

Painfully injure knuckles punching table in puerile fit of frustration.

Cat visibly frightened.

Commence softly weeping.

Drool a bit. Nose drips viscous spidery skeins.

Experience abrupt epiphany! — Of course! —

Loving-kindness is the only way!

Tear down Tony Robbins-type Post-its and replace with new ones

parrotting inspirational Buddhist bumper stickers

seen on beat-up biodiesel vans parked at farmers' market.

Feel much better now. Wipe away tears and sort of

laugh and cry at same time.

Thank God no one witnessed this.

Cat still hungry. Clap hands loudly, stomp floor and yell

"Give me a minute, you little fuck!"

Realize that was a trifle too loud and now the really nice

young couple next door,

who clearly already wonder about you,

have yet another reason to always give a wide berth

and only the briefest of cursory hellos.

Distractedly wonder if maybe they think you're gay.

Instantly recognize the lame inanity

and implicit homophobia of this thought.

Cynically declaim, "Oh, that's just great, you shallow prick."

Apologize to cat. Open can of two-dollar-fifty hypoallergenic
wet food made from rabbits prescribed by vet.
Hope the rabbits are being killed for some other reason
and cat food is made from extraneous killing process by-products
because killing scores of rabbits
to feed one chronically malcontent sixteen-year-old feline
just doesn't seem right.
Numbly take down loving-kindness Post-its and give up.
Suddenly remember imminent arrival of Latino roofing crew.
Tense up and draw blinds immediately.
Tell self it does no good
to feel ashamed, embarrassed, and a trifle effeminate
to be flouncing in and out all day while they labor in the hot sun
casting quizzical glances in your direction as you come and go.
Resolve to ostentatiously tote your Lil' Playmate
working man's lunch cooler with you
when you go out,
making sure they see you're just like them,
perhaps calling out jauntily "*Saludos amigos!*"
then just stay at the library all day until they're gone.
Pour more coffee, absently pet cat, and peripherally notice
teeming column of defiant, savage ants brazenly assaulting garbage.
Let head drop with a resigned shake.
Grit teeth and whimper like an injured puppy.
Turn out all lights, cue up Lou Reed CD and crawl into bed

with the sound of ladders being thrown against the building
and the roofers all mundanely conversing with each other
in perfect, unaccented English.

.

AFTER THE PARTY

Tonight I share my childhood bed

with my adult wife

same looming trees peering in

scraping the glass

still behaving poorly

the same moon

throwing its neutral shadows

open to interpretation

the same windy creeks and groans

tireless and bothersome

asking their repetitive questions

She'll dream deeply there

immune   impervious

to my insomniac sojourn

down vigil halls

tiptoeing past my father's chamber

sidestepping the sentry floorboard

still creaking its warnings

descending darkened stairs

eight

a landing   left turn

nine to the bottom

no light down here

thirty years later

in my boyhood

silent and vast

the rooms vacant tonight

feigning un-recognition

of this tentative intruder

but they do

feel my heat   my singular pulse

the indelible taste

of the palpable humors

I breathed and sweated and cried

and laughed

here inside these walls

they know me

and remember well

things we both have dismissed

stored in the attic   the basement

left to gather dust

Returning to my love

breathing slow and deep there

I close the door

Amidst the subtle language

of bricks and pipes and timbers

ghostly white noise

layers of it

deafening fragments

floating echoes ricocheting lonely

settling on my skin

resting and quiet

glad for familiar company

the years whispering away

up the chimney

PEOPLE I FEEL SORRY FOR

Women whose nipples are constantly, disconcertingly erect—

willful, cold-in-any-climate, bra-busting, I.Q.-dropping, king-size, Ju Ju Bee nipples.

I believe we must begin here.

Certainly deserving of consideration are those intrepid unfortunates

(most assuredly underpaid)

who courageously pilot a sickeningly reeking truck

just brimming with anonymous, miscegenating turds all day long,

inadequately clad in rubber boots and gloves,

repeatedly thrusting an unwieldy turbo-sucking corrugated hose

deep into a putrid Stygian abyss

(wherein placidly lurks my own personal version of Hell)

all in an unstably wobbling fly-infested blue plastic shit-house

positively baking in the kiln-like July inferno,

(we all know the asphyxiating, claustrophobic, "God, please don't let my genitals touch any part of this God-forsaken venereal Petri-shack, I swear I'll be good forever" feeling)

at the blue-grass festival,

or the county fair,

or the local 10-K,

or heaven forbid the medievally disconcerting Sturgis Biker Rally. Horrifying stuff.

We all feel sorry for those worn-out middle-aged couples

we see in restaurants

who long ago exhausted their lifetime's ration of conversation.

"I wonder how the scallops are?" she brightly offers.

"Mmm," he drones, without looking up from his menu.

She manipulates her ring in circles around her finger,

clears her throat and smiles half-heartedly at the busboy.

He inaudibly sighs, brow inscrutably furrowed,

lowers his menu and stares off vacantly, like a guy doing time.

Sad.

But consider our poor nipple-woman.

Half the world is mesmerically unable to process even her simplest
utterance.

Coretta Scott King could be delivering a soaring, soul-stirring sequel to

"I Have A Dream,"

but if those hypnotic hi-beams are on,

all of those multi-racial, beautiful, brotherly loving men

beatifically co-existing on the august, sparkling Washington Mall,

would just be gently elbowing each other,

leaning over slightly, going

"Brother, what'd she just say?"

"Search me, dude."

It's not fair.

Ted-X weenies, Hare Krishnas, Log Cabin Republicans, race-walkers,

people who have those frothy white saliva strings

at the corner of their mouths when they talk,

folks whose chili gets ignored at the pot-luck

when the chili right next door is all gone.

First base coaches, tambourine players, exfoliators.

Anybody stupid enough to get a tattoo of their boyfriend or girl-friend's name.

Proctologists, phlebotomists, ventriloquists, snake-milkers, sword-swallowers, fluffers, women named Gertrude or Mildred, grown men cursed with little-boy peckers.

Meg Ryan for God's sake!

Why Meg, why?!

Another category: metal-detector misanthropes

(actually, I secretly yearn to metal-detect.

It's a freaking treasure hunt,

and you can skulk right up next to young women in bikinis,

yet you're practically invisible.

It's like a cloaking device for middle-aged men.).

Still, nothing says "My life is fundamentally over" like a metal detector.

Those of you who purchased a Chevy Volt have my sympathy.

I mean, you were being doubly virtuous.

Not just a hybrid,

but American-made as well.

Little did you know you were essentially buying a modern-day Pinto,

only this time with an electronic pilot light.

I thought I felt sorry for those ridiculous sorts who participate in two-man luge.

Have you seen this?

One man lies belly-up on a tiny sled,

clad in one of those ultra-snug space-age body condoms,

and his partner then lies there as well,

right on top of him,

belly-up too.

Down the course they plummet.

How silly!

"Hah, hah" I laugh derisively.

One fit, muscular man, lying right on top of the other,

careening together down the course at thrilling speeds

—over and over.

Prone, right on top of each other.

Right fucking on top.

Hanging desperately on for dear life.

Two hearts adrenally pulsing as one,

irresistible G-forces

pressing you tightly into one another with each undulating curve…

What is wrong with me!!?

I don't feel sorry for these guys, I envy them.

Pity me then.

An ostensibly straight man

who finds himself surprisingly excited by the thought of two-man luge

(this is not the first time something like this has come up, so to speak).

Afraid to approach unfamiliar women, on-line date, drunk-dial an old flame,

or purchase even the mildest of porn.

Perhaps then it's finally time to head to Big 5

and invest in that high resolution, full spectrum imaging, Commando 4,000 metal detector,

one of those "I'm a dork and I don't care," Lawrence of Arabia sun-hats with all the flaps,

and a vest with lots of pockets and zippers,

and definitely one of those cool sifter baskets

with the long handle that those guys employ to glean all the goodies.

And maybe some galoshes too,

'cause that's just how I roll.

Hey Ladies! See you on the beach!

I DON'T GET IT

Raw cauliflower—loathsome, flatulence-inducing weed.

no flavor, aesthetically disastrous.

Masticated, it renders

into tiny, cough-inducing micro-particles.

Why then, allow it on the tray

with all the likable vegetables

at festive gatherings?

Red peppers, cherry tomatoes, mini-carrots, celery

maybe even a small sprig of broccoli

with a big enough glob of ranch dressing—okay,

but please, no more cauliflower.

I don't get conga lines, the bunny hop, or the hokey pokey.

Fascistic, conformist exercises in choreographed buffoonery

doesn't matter if it's a wedding, a cruise ship, or an old folks home

you can't help but appear

a goonishly grinning mental defective.

I don't understand how cats get enough air through those tiny pin-hole nostrils,

why moths can't fly straight

and why snakes don't have legs.

Actually, I see no valid reason for snakes at all.

Ireland does just fine without them,

but then they're cursed with bagpipes

which may in fact be worse.

I'll never understand the Riverdance, Catholicism, James Joyce,

optional oral hygiene, or kilts.

It's a skirt. For God's sake, please, just call it that.

I don't understand Shakespeare at all, literally.

What on earth are those ridiculous drama pussies talking about?

Gooey French cheese that costs twenty dollars a pound

and smells like an Athens cabbie's rancidly pungent ass-crack.

Come on, nobody's that hungry.

And why do baseball coaches need to wear uniforms

and continually pat everybody on the ass?

Why are the players so obsessed with their crotches?

All this simian grabbing and tugging.

Why can't they get things organized down there

and then just play the damn game?

And speaking of grown men and uniforms,

those scout-leader types,

with their too-short shorts, hairless legs, and weird neckerchiefs

really freak me out.

Keep your fucking merit badges to yourself,

if you know what I mean.

But what I really don't get,

and I hope I'm not alone here,

is why they need to make condoms so maddeningly large.

No, not the Magnums, the regular ones.

I'm like a little kid clomping around in his dad's loafers.

Does anybody else have trouble keeping those emasculating things on?

I mean, how are you supposed to maintain a class one erection

while obsessively worrying about condom slippage?

And let's just say it—briefs are far more functional than boxers.

The only reason to wear boxers is because no woman gets turned on

by a guy standing there looking like a giant seven-year-old

with pee stains where the magic is supposed to be happening.

I also often wonder why footloose twenty-something women,

the ones with the yoga mats, the soul-melting lacquered-on fuchsia tights,

the disorienting, unfair navel piercings,

who seem to not even notice you as you hold the door,

don't find themselves somehow devil-may-carishly drawn

(okay, just the ones with Daddy issues)

to quirky, dyspeptic, yellow-toothed, penny-pinching, cat fancying, briefs-wearing,

questionably endowed, middle-aged men.

And please explain to me again why couples therapists charge $150 an hour

just to say, "Tell me more about that, Jenn"

and,

"Pete, please, it's Jenn's turn to talk right now"

and,

"Pete, do you hear what Jenn is saying?

It's important that you really try to listen here."

But then she just up and divorces your mystified ass anyway.

What The Hell?!

And lately, I've been wondering how come I think you could just

blow off the front of this crummy apartment

and cover it with plexiglass,

and it would be like a museum diorama, with one of those plaques out front

that reads:

"Archetypal bitterly confused mateless misanthrope. Commonly found ruefully muttering to self and gesturing to unseen companion in frozen food aisle of local Trader Joe's. Prone to wistfully leafing through old photo albums and periodically emitting audible regret-laden sighs."

And passersby could look in and point and exclaim

in tones of real heartfelt wonder,

"I don't understand how come that poor slob doesn't just lose his freaking mind in there."

Fucking know-it-alls.

Why people can't just mind their own damn business is beyond me.

WITH APOLOGIES TO SCARF PEOPLE

At the hipster café the radiant woman-child

quizzically inspected my chipped, handleless mug.

"It's so small"

she remarked with a curious tilt of the head

"I hate it when women say that"

I so drolly replied.

She sparkled with demure laughter, said it was on the house.

I tipped her four bits. Sinatra I am not.

I took a seat and cracked open my nemesis

The Vintage Book of Contemporary American Poetry—

weighty fare—love, death, betrayal, despair,

soothsaying clouds, breezes fraught with meaning,

portentous helicoptering autumn leaves,

plangent and grave meditations on decay, regret…more despair.

"I must write of these matters"

I thought, leafing absently through the sports page.

"I wish to be taken seriously" I told myself

while secretly eyeing succulent woman-child barista

stretch oh so luxuriantly upward, hands raised like a diver

the arched back, the exposed midriff…I digress…

For am I not an artist, after all?

Profound and tortured and complex…

Oh to wear dark clothing and scarves, geometrically shaped,

pretentiously tinted eyeglasses, turtlenecks even.

To sip espresso effetely

as I gesture expansively with a smoldering foreign cigarette

to laughingly dismiss ideas as pedestrian

when I really don't understand them at all,

to confidently enunciate the word 'bourgeoisie'

with nary a trace of irony.

I must have stormy, exhaustive relationships—

she is beautiful and troubled, of course,

we fight like passionate starving wolves

Central American politics, gender identity, *Finnegan's Wake*,

the infield fly rule…

The sex is amazing…lots of candles and dramatic shadows,

incense, aboriginal music.

She has a bewitching accent. I believe she's Israeli—

served in the military, knows karate, speaks four languages,

currently on some sort of academic fellowship…

No.

No way that woman even looks my way,

turtleneck or not.

Okay. So I'm a misunderstood iconoclastic genius,

a brooding combative solitary creator, alone in the world, defiantly so.

A celibate rebel with a poetic cause,

who watches porn every afternoon at three.

(I always seem to come right when the mailman does)

Yet, woman or not, I must boldly sound

the dialectical depths of the existentially unfathomable.

(insouciantly sporting a jaunty beret as I do so).

Clearly unwise in the ways of love,

I shamelessly plagiarize Tokugawa-era romance haiku.

Oh, people love the spare elegance, the unrequited yearnings,

the stoical acceptance of my lonely lot,

the ubiquitous cherry blossoms…

(here I don a fetchingly mid-thigh apricot kimono for ethno-sartorial inspiration)

As for death, I mine the cinematic,

Russell Crowe slowly expiring on the Colosseum floor,

poisoned by River Phoenix's hissing brother.

Gauzy dreamlike visions of his wife, his child, his horse,

as he draws his final dramatic breaths.

Oh Maximus,

oh noble gladiator,

why do I so yearn to be your lissome young stable boy?

(My writerly apparel in this case a tasteful everyman's toga and sensibly strappy sandals).

Of this I so earnestly write,

greedily sucking the marrow

from the bones of lovelorn Japanese bards

and maudlin Hollywood clichés.

Does my mendacity injure? Shall I forever hold my duplicitous peace?

When I read this dreck at the community center workshop

the artistes man-hug me.

"I'm proud of you bro" they croak hoarsely,

holding on a bit too long for my liking.

Strangely garbed women named Luna,

who paint badly and read Tarot

buy me chai and hold my hand—

tell me I have an old soul.

Oh, Great Good Heavens!!

I should have realized this years ago—

quoting Nietzsche in German even,

obscure and implicitly snotty Greek mythology references:

heartbreak and death and suffering,

not constipation and crabs and a bulimic cat.

Oh, you silly silver-maned adolescent

to what do you cling?

Your fatuous fellows await.

Get it over with already.

Just go ahead and buy some surplus Soviet army boots,

a properly proletarian pair of woolen trousers,

a carton of Gauloise, a rakish hat, a dog-eared early edition *Ulysses,*

and that tasseled magenta symphony conductor scarf

you so secretly yearn to affect.

You never know,

you just might like it.

TRUE FRIENDSHIP

You can't write if the correct energy's not there.

And today I clearly don't have it.

Yet here you and I sit, engaged in this one-way conversation,

which is actually how I prefer it, when it's just you and me.

Because when you're talking, I act like I'm listening—Oh,

I nod, maintain eye contact, laugh half-heartedly when you do,

ask inane leading questions which I almost instantly regret.

But I'm really somewhere else.

Somewhere estranged, creepingly nihilistic, existentially defeated.

You see, I absolutely do not give one steaming shit, not a rat's pink shiny ass,

about that scenic Napa Valley half marathon you've been training for,

or your uncle's unfortunate recent colonoscopy,

or your well-considered thoughts on the whole thorny immigration issue—

you know—you can really see both sides, it's all so complex—

NAFTA, human rights, free trade, Paul Krugman, Horatio Alger, Sonia Sotomayor—

Oh please stop!

Then it strangles out "You bore me! Yes! Hah! There, I said it, to fidgety fucking tears."

God, how good does <u>that</u> feel?! What a freaking load off.

But hey, don't take it personal. It had to be said. Ask anybody.

Imagine if you could just simply declare that ugly reality to people,
devoid of rancor, just the unmoving truth, in all its fulsome glory,
and then just walk away.
Tough love at its finest.
Hopefully, just maybe—a lone hanging light bulb dimly incandesces.
The rusted tumblers all slowly click into place.
"You know what? He's right. I really am a tedious motherfucker.
Everything I think and say parrots various media sources—
an amalgam of borrowed ideas—highbrow or lowbrow, it doesn't matter.
I really like to quote Malcolm Gladwell, Ted X, and of course NPR.
People seem to really respect that.
"Did you hear Barbara Ehrenreich on Fresh Air last night?"
But I'm really afraid to say what it is I actually believe.
I'm not even sure what that is, come to think of it.
I just want people to think well of me.
I want to be accepted and liked... Is that so wrong?"
There, doesn't that feel better?
Now, let's have the rest. Unvarnished.

So, you really dig your daughter's second grade teacher.
I thought so. I just knew it.
You love your wife and all, but why do you so look forward
to open house, parent-teacher conferences, field trips?
Why always solicitously volunteering to pick up the kids?
Such newfound vigor, such bright-eyed paternal enthusiasm.
Hey, I don't blame you,

she's a hot, single, twenty-nine-year old with a heart of gold and
perfect teeth.

That time you ran into her at the beach,

elegantly sipping a Corona and reading Erica Jong—Ooh.

That hidden hip tattoo—a rose, you think—you didn't want to stare.

That surprisingly erotic navel-piercing, gleaming like treasure itself

when she languidly rolled up to face you,

the sun suddenly hotter on your back.

All by herself. God, you just wanted to abandon the kids

and lay down right there next to her and

wallow unrepentantly in her very aroma, her affectless joy.

And when she laughed at what you said,

threw back her pony-tailed head and really cut loose

that balmy evening in Whole Foods,

surrounded by mangoes and papayas, her playful hand

unexpectedly on your shoulder.

Did it linger there? What was her intent?

Oh, probably nothing.

Would it be wrong to invite her to an innocent coffee sometime,

maybe on the other side of town?

Probably so, yes, definitely.

But now, when you're biblically with your wife, whom you indeed
love very much,

and I can see why,

you're clearly visualizing, it's almost holographic—

Miss Honeycutt, in leather, in the classroom,

poutishly scolding you for thinking your nasty little thoughts.

You've been having sex lately with greater frequency and fervor than you have in years,

and the wife is going along more or less willingly,

although she does occasionally request

that you open your eyes from time to time and actually look at her.

She seems somehow bemused by it all.

Leggy, freckled, auburn-haired, shoulder-touching Miss Honeycutt.

      Candice, her name is. Candice…

What else, what else? This is getting interesting.

I'm actually starting to like you… What's that?

You're sick of seeing homeless white males

pathetically begging for change in the nicer shopping areas?

Me too! Me too!

I understand: women, children, the mentally ill, the infirm, vets with PTSD, etc.

It's tragic, tragic. We'd like to help, we're not heartless, you and I,

but these bums—yes, that's what they are—say it, say it—

these scumbags, these losers, vermin—

Oh, now we're getting somewhere!

They don't want jobs, they just want a free ride.

Hacky-sack my taxpaying ass.

Those twirly sticks, the sad puppies, they can't even take care of themselves—

why the flea-bitten, undernourished puppies?

"Get a job" if you want to spit—who doesn't? You stare them down.

Defiantly, they glare right back.

You're pretty sure you could kick their ass, if it ever came right down to it.

But let's talk about your wife, a woman of rare quality and charm,

as I can truly attest.

But it's two and a half years now since kid #2 dropped,

and she's still packing that extra twenty pounds.

Not ten, but twenty rather cellulitic pounds.

Thank God for Miss Honeycutt.

Would it kill her to do more than just walk for exercise?

You're working full time, and preparing for a half marathon,

not a 10-K, 13.1 hot, hilly, wine-country miles.

But she just walks and yammers with that shrewish Beth Adler-Abramson,

Bethany, excuse me, the part-time family therapist.

You wish they'd never met, don't you?

That's what you get for doing Lamaze, Mr. Sensitive.

What a bunch of pussy-whipped losers in <u>that</u> bunch.

But you were one of them! Ha! Weren't you?

Remember college in Santa Barbara?

The co-ed ultimate team. It was practically a roaming orgy—

tents, sleeping bags, cheap wine, taut, willing bodies still salty from running all day…

Yes, yes—better to put that out of your head—I agree.

But Constance spoils those kids rotten.

And the names—Delilah and Quincy. How precious, how affected—

keeping up with the progressive, Prius-driving Joneses,

even when it comes to picking children's names.

Henry and Sarah you wanted. Ah well, pick your battles, pick your battles.

But for Pete's sake pick one, any one!

She'd actually respect you more.

This is what she tells Beth, it's true.

It's what she tells me, too, when we're together.

Yes, the jig is up! Honesty it is!

There's a reason she's not so into sex any more.

That whole yoga class she started attending recently,

the Title IX sportswear, the mat, the high-end water bottle?

It's just a ruse.

Yoga, schmoga—she's with me—downward doggy style!

And I actually prefer zaftig, Rubenesque women—

more cushion, you know.

Yes, the black guys are right about that. Shit, they're right about practically everything.

We do things you've never even heard of!

She actually told me she'd like to try a threesome next.

She's making subtle entreaties already—

me, her, and, get this—Candice Honeycutt!

I know, I know—I couldn't believe it either!

Man, I can hardly wait.

Oh. Sorry. I just thought it was important to be honest.

BEGGARS CAN'T BE CHOOSERS, BUT HERE I GO ANYWAY

Clearly the author of these words is no prize.

As has been more lucidly, or perhaps hopefully

more compellingly articulated in his quite limited

ramblings elsewhere, which an audience in the

mid to high double digit range (maybe 65 to 75, he hopes)

has kindly tolerated, we have seen time

and poetic time again said author manifesting

a melange of traits both antisocial and

pathologically self-defeating which render him

largely undesirable to the female of the species.

Indeed, an anxiety-ridden, likely Asperger afflicted,

mother-resenting, unemployed middle-aged compulsive

vacuum jockey who obsesses over comely

grocery checkers half his age, plays dissonant unsettling

middle-school level trumpet, employs arcane Renaissance

era grooming practices and leads an entirely

cat-centric existence is in no way shape or form

entitled to label any kettle as black or throw even

the tiniest of pebbles within the troubled confines

of his squalid little glass apartment.

That being said the sad scribbler invokes the license

artistic and forthwith presents an incomplete yet

highly nuanced encapsulation of traits, proclivities,

and appetites which necessarily categorize certain of the fairer

persuasion as largely unfit for pursuit by, or cohabitation

with, said humble, misanthropic, some day to be

self-published scribe. To wit: I, Peter (last name

withheld for obvious reasons) will not date,

indeed will in fact, except in certain sordid

desperate circumstances, shun all such women

as herein elucidated;

Women who perform in improv troops

Women who share my mother's first name

Women whose pet of choice slithers legless and feasts with forked tongue on innocent bamboozled rodents, sick women who by logical conclusion actually enjoy procuring and sacrificing said sloe-eyed creatures and raptly witnessing the brutal primal spectacle of nightmarish herpetic predator and unwitting mammalian prey. Disgusting.

Women who listen to Kenny G

Women who practice Wicca

Women who take forever to order and ask all sorts of show-offy foodie questions, or worse yet, attempt to order off the menu entirely.

Women who begin statements with, "I was listening to NPR the other day. . ."

Women who do all that wine-tasting sniffing and swishing around bullshit

Bare with me, I'm just getting started here…

Women who think it's important to have a job or at least set some goals

Women who have an ex-husband with a restraining order, a parole officer, or have ever taken part in any sort of conjugal visit

Women who are considering changing their name to Sparklehawk Wind-catcher

Women who drive obliviously under the speed limit in the fast lane while telling that same tired story about that time at Burning Man - "Oh my God, you should have seen us!"

Women who for any reason mention Deepak Chopra

Women who participate in Toastmasters, Scientology, or cock-fighting

Women who ever lived in a trailer down by the river with a self-employed taxidermist named Skeeter

Women who suggest that perhaps an iron supplement or multi-vitamin might help my sexual stamina - of course this is just a fun poem, I really don't have problems in that department, or at least that's how I remember it, anyway.

Women who attended Waldorf or Montessori school

Women who own a massive pit bull named Beelzebub with intact testicles and a spiky leather collar with dripping red pentagrams painted on it

Women who become hyper-animated when extolling the myriad virtues of hemp

Women who wear Google Glasses or even just one of those self-important earpiece things and walk down the street talking too loud and gesturing emphatically — Don't they know they look fucking crazy!?

(Deep Breath)

Women who have mug shot or know anyone named Bam-Bam,

Spider, or Blade

Women who eat pastry with a knife and fork

Women who say irregardless – it's not a word, it's just not a fucking word, okay?!

Women who want me to join their ex-husband's shamanic vision quest drum circle, sweat lodge group

Women who take their teeth out at bedtime

Women who dance the robot or play the didgereedoo

Women who quite energetically attempt to insert an emasculating finger into my quivering, reluctant rectum during the physical act of coitus

Women who ask me if I think Jennifer Aniston will ever find love as we lie in bed reading our periodicals of choice

Women who object to my Avant-Garde David Byrnish dance style which in the past has garnered unsolicited comments such as "Where do you dance?"

Women who don't fake orgasms well, and if you can't fake the orgasm, please just look up at me all bug-eyed like I'm some kind of virile marauding pirate right as I'm about to come

Women with a cat named Mr. Fiddlesticks or some stupid shit like that who have a menagerie of stuffed animals on their bed

Women who speak French

Women who know how to make cotton candy, drink 64 ounce Big Gulps and smoke extra long menthol cigarettes

Women who plead longingly to pop my zits

Women who don't understand – I really DO want them to stick their finger up there –

I just like playing hard to get.

GOOD LORD, I MIGHT BE GAY

6:51 am and already the day an unqualified success.

Percussive, mortar-like auto erotic orgasm

achieved immediately upon waking

employing left-handed reverse grip tambourine shake method.

Absence from masturbatory mental imagery

of firefighter ex-wife and alarmingly well hung colleagues

engaging in stunningly spirited sexual hijinks

a tremendous relief.

Surprise cameo by strapping young mystery man

recently encountered at local art gallery open house,

perhaps best described as a more muscular

George Michael from the early Wham! years

(minus, of course, the unduly garish pastel exercise togs)

initially disconcerting,

however upon at least temporary abandonment

of traditional hetero-centric psycho-sexual dogma

and subsequent surprisingly facile full-throttle

immersion in steamy health club sauna

fellatial dreamscape scenario

gratefully resurrected phallus

responded in positively equine fashion,

bucking and braying like a wild rutting stallion,

rising majestically to his full, proud five and thirteen sixteenths of an inch height

(depending, of course, upon where you measure from. . .)

True story:

When I was fourteen, a handsome young male nurse

was tasked with placing my newly capricious genitals

into a protective pouch made of lead.

I had fractured my femur

and required an x-ray.

As he touched me there,

my starving member sprang to attention.

No flag pull was ever more resolute.

For a moment, he grappled with the stalwart appendage,

but it would bend to no will but its own.

"I'll come back when you've calmed down"

he said.

It's not like I think about it much,

but what if that man had tenderly covered my young mouth with his,

smoothly stroked me off,

as I've no doubt he had countless other men before?

Would I have innocently acceded?

Would I have awkwardly reciprocated?

Good Lord!

Is that a fattening I feel

in my moribund manhood as I write this?

Certainly something tingly is going on down there.

Should I be barking up an entirely different tree?

And if so, will I need better clothes?

After shave? Depilatory utensils?

Yes, I linger lustfully over those glossy advertisements

featuring a shirtlessly scowling David Beckham.

Who doesn't?! The man is beautiful!

Yes! As a small boy I played a thrilling game

called "Joe Namath" with my best friend,

in which one of us would enact

the masculine role of Broadway Joe,

the other

an all too willing stewardess or shop girl.

Yes, that same little boy and I choreographed

lengthy sophisticated musical numbers

which we would effervescently perform

before his gleefully applauding sisters.

Oh, it's all too much, too confusing.

I think I'll go down

this sweltering afternoon

to the local library

and check out that fabulous oversize

body-building primer that I so enjoy.

Those gorgeous rippling Adonises all seem so cocksure

so incandescently virile

clad only in a Speedo and dazzling smile,

so brimming over with unfettered masculinity.
Why, one can almost smell the pungent briny aroma
of their throbbing mannish exertions
wafting tantalizingly up from the page.

Ah, to have been a servile young towel boy
perhaps by the darkly intriguing name of Raoul Fonseca,
haunting sylph-like
the musky men's locker room
of the legendary Venice Beach Gold's, circa 1983,
stealing sotto voce into a complicit broom closet
with a guileless green-eyed Romanian muscle man
fresh off the boat, hungry for life,
famished, yet bursting. . .

Hey, a guy can dream a little, can't he?

NORTH BEACH CHICKEN

Every day I do the same shit
I drink coffee
and make resolutions
"Today is the first day of…"
Good God
by midafternoon I'm wondering
where and when
it all went so wrong
finally
I believe I have the answer
Mill Valley, summer, 1995
she was so hot
that balmy evening in the 2 a.m. club
honey-blonde hair, just-so jeans
and mischievous, clever hands
she was married
but that didn't stop us
Boy Oh Boy
right there on my best friend's
living room rug
can you imagine?
I felt like George Clooney
Two years later

she was telling me

her tone weary and frustrated

that if I didn't come

to terms with my feelings

about my mother

we could never achieve true intimacy

OH NO!!

It was in a restaurant

North Beach, Columbus Ave

they served only roast chicken

with potatoes to die for

the tables were really close together

this sad lonely guy

reading science fiction (I'm pretty sure it was Dune)

had no choice but to overhear

I mean, he was literally two feet away

I said, quite reasonably, I thought

"Could we discuss this later? In private?"

She fumed, picked at her food

"Are you gonna eat those fries?" I asked,

unable to help myself

(they were that good)

that was the beginning

as they say

of the end

it didn't work out

I married someone else
who also knew in great depth
just what was wrong with me.
Now I sit here
mystified, bereft, bamboozled even
my ex-wife's cat
somehow in my possession
demanding his customary share
of my Sunday scrambled eggs

I pray nowadays
for a buxom woman
of dubious character
to enter my life
somehow
turn everything deliciously
upside-down.

Needless to say
I never did work through
those issues with mother.

THE HORROR

Dear reader

Oh heartfelt confidant

my secrets

like jagged kidney stones

must be passed, released, scrutinized

no matter the pain, the scabrous indignity

true healing requires it

so with your kind permission

I purge myself here and now.

Gape, in enthralled titillation

or avert your modest gaze.

Regardless

Schadenfreude awaits. . .

A utilitarian examining room

almost second-world

for all its shabbiness

faded posters

encouraging salubrious behaviors

crudely scotch-taped

curling at the edges, yellowing

a recalcitrant fluorescent bulb

flickering above

as though mocking

this my ghastly predicament

terrified

of an untimely erection

my eyes bloodshot, thoughts scattered

a hunchbacked octogenarian

female MD

wielding in her palsied claw

a preposterous Sherlock Holmes

magnifying glass

close over my thankfully dormant manhood

"Yup, you've got crabs all right"

she declared matter-of-factly,

almost triumphantly, it seemed

turning abruptly away

as she scribbled out the prescription,

her geriatric scrawl illegible –

the crone.

But the troubles fester

my embarrassment metastasizes

for you see

the causative carnal act

was never consummated.

"How? How can this be?" you gasp.

But first, close your eyes
picture, if you will
the look of bored disgust
traumatizingly evident
on the face of the bespectacled
matronly Walgreen's cashier
as she rang up the total
the price to be paid
for the poison, nay, the insecticide
Quell, its all too descriptive moniker
I would soon vigorously lather
deep into the "infested area"
this nightmare, this Kurtzian Hell
crawling and alive
between my tender thighs.
Oh, the horror indeed.

Returning to the initiatory tryst
the inept nocturnal fumblings
the close alcoholic breathing
the dorm room single bed gymnastics
oh, if those mute cinder block walls
could but testify
they would bear sober witness
to my futile drunken feebleness

at the moment of truth

my vaunted love shaft

but a pathetic pink slinky

helplessly flopping this way and that

searching frantically for Heaven's elusive gate,

expiring limply

as she moaned in throaty anticipation

of what would never come.

I lay there, deflated in the darkness

her consoling murmurs

but faint solace

her snoring soon thereafter

unconsciously degrading.

I remember not

whether I remained

or slunk home in the gloaming

the fog of memory mercifully obscures.

Yet on days

when jock-itch unbidden

rears its dry, psoriatic head,

like a shell-shocked soldier

triggered by a sudden backfire

I am whisked to the past,

visions, haunting and terrible

of the wild-eyed little beasts

scrambling madly to and fro

bits of crimson flesh

dangling from their savage maws

my besieged loins

aflame

my throbbing young heart

broken.

I VACUUM A LOT

No computer, no cell phone, no TV,
No woman, no job,
So I vacuum a lot.

The dirt-catching box is removable
So I empty it after each use
I think I get better suction that way
It's important to stay hydrated
So I always keep a glass of water handy
My cat has fleas
Sometimes when I vacuum
I see them trapped in the transparent
Green plastic of the dirt-catching box
It feels good knowing
They won't be jumping on him.
If the phone rings
While I am vacuuming
I don't hear it
But then that light is flashing
—playing phone tag with mother is fun—
My new vacuum is quieter
Than the old one
So the cat doesn't run like crazy

Until the very last moment

He's like a streak of gray fur

The old one stopped sucking

So I took it apart,

Then I threw all that

Stuff away

I do laundry a lot

And I keep everything

Well folded in the appropriate drawer

Occasionally I tip up the mattress

And vacuum under the bed

But it's pretty clean under there

I always try to greet the mailman

"No mail today" he says

I wonder what kind

Of sunscreen he uses

I'm pretty sure my neighbors

Hear the vacuum and wonder

If I'm crazy or maybe have OCD

That's okay with me

I'm pretty sure it's OCD

I always vacuum in the same pattern

It usually takes six or seven minutes

I don't know why it's different sometimes

I go to Trader Joe's right

When it opens

So there is no trouble with parking

Sometimes I go while

The laundry is drying

Killing two birds you know

I pay the phone bill in person

That way there's no mix-ups

My vet said vacuuming vibrates

Things and makes flea eggs hatch

But I think between the

Vacuuming and combing him every day

It keeps them under control

I'm thinking of changing vets

I always set up the coffee

Maker the night before

When the cat wakes me up

I walk over and press

The button

By the time I'm dressed

Presto—fresh hot coffee

I have two cups at the end

Of cup number one I sweep

The kitchen floor and clean

The cat box and make the bed

I never vacuum before eight

Two scrambled eggs toast and a banana

And I'm ready to go

Time for an oil change

Says the sticker on my windshield

So I call and set up

An appointment

Three thousand miles sure go by fast

I make sure to always

Have plenty of light bulbs and an

Assortment of batteries on hand

Just in case

I like not getting caught

With no vacuum cleaner bags

Since my new vacuum

Doesn't even use them

I don't have to worry about that

Anymore.

CUBA LIBRE

Mi Corazón ya vive
en la Habana de mis sueños
veo las palmas, la playa tan blanca, el cielo azul
huelo el olor de arroz con pollo
volando sobre las brisas tropicales
oigo abuelas platicando en la calle como pájaros…
so commences the opening stanza
of the enrapturing new work
that with any luck
if there is indeed justice
in the wicked world
will somehow get me some action.
It has to. Oh Ese, it must.
If a sensitive work, a poignant remembrance
half in Spanish, half English
of my halcyon years abroad
con la gente de Cuba
won't motivate at least one comely, misguided
Bohemian boomer body worker
to waste an amorous evening or three on me
I give up. *No más. Ya no quiero vivir.*
Oh, I'll incorporate heady imagery
about Che, Fidel, Teófiol Stevenson,
and those colorful old jalopies

nosing carefully about Havana—
azure waves crashing against the seawall
spraying those bemused, ancient Spanish cobbles.
I'll wax rhapsodic
about my work in a one room school house
far in the country, among the Guajiros
cleaving meaty, milky coconuts
with my trusty machete
sipping hot café in the chill morning air…
Of course, I've never actually
been to Cuba.
I've only been to Watsonville
once or twice.
But I can't write another word
about the stultifying existence
I am currently choking on
here in Santa Cruz.
Denied a free Whopper Junior by a pimply-faced teen in a paper hat
because my coupon expired yesterday.
Every morning stepping stiffly
into one of my three pairs of irregular Dockers,
today, sexless pleatedless beige.
My battered tennis shoes waiting like death,
stinking of decay and Tinactin.
Standing in line at the DMV, browsing at Ross,
five dollar foot-longs at Subway.
Half for lunch, the other for dinner.

Working out at the playground,
Pull-ups and such…
Being aggressively accosted
By upscale helicopter parents
who judge me a probable pedophile.
Pirating cable TV, secretly reading the Enquirer at CVS
getting ripped off at Jiffy Lube again.
Fallen arches, yellow teeth, blue balls, ear hair like wire,
too cheap to pay for a haircut
a sit-down restaurant
a full tank of gas
tickets to anything.
Addicted to SportsCenter
a slave to my cat
still angry at my mother—
she's seventy-six fucking years old
for Christ's sake.
Por favor, allow me one
Advanced Placement Spanish poem
about *revolución y el mar y mi vida Cubana.*
Consider me a magic realist,
not a desperate fraud.
And if you see me at the farmer's market,
hand in hand with my new hippie honey,
feeding each other organic strawberries
and sharing some inside joke,
amigo.
¡Cállate!

TMI

Strangling a frightened sea cucumber
was the most apt metaphor I could conjure up
when describing to an indulgently good-humored female friend
the lamentably arduous indignity
that is middle-aged male masturbation.

Goodness, she laughed—a retired firefighter,
she enjoys such ribald humor, bless her tolerant soul.
But that's what it's like nowadays.
Or perhaps a luckless gold prospector,
flogging a recalcitrant sway-backed donkey up a hill.
The honking beast ultimately pulls the load
but it's a chore for all involved,
and there's really no gold to be found
in that dismal pile of laboriously extracted loam.
Is this more than you wish to hear?
Then I'll stop for a moment and you can leave.
I don't blame you.
It only gets worse.
Here's the funny-sad part
I do it lefty these days—I'll explain momentarily.
But just try signing your name,
sketching a random barnyard animal,

describing a simple circle

with your uncoordinated hand,

it's a spastic mess, indecipherable and disconcerting.

Welcome to my auto-not so very erotic world.

You see, my right arm is somewhat atrophied

due to a troubling inability to remain rubber-side down

as both a competitive cyclist and triathlete.

Oh, the hospital bills, the massive radiation from X-rays, CT scans

two medevac helicopter rides for God's sake.

The wrist thrice-broken, collarbone once, half a dozen ribs, a punc-
tured lung even,

forearm snapped in two—a plate and six screws forever.

That arm will never be the same.

I play a hobbyist's trumpet, just on the passable side of annoying

but that's a not inconsequential right arm workout—try it sometime

same with my 5-speed manual Honda—shifting, shifting, always
shifting.

My vanity compels me to lift weights twice a week, so more overuse,

but worst of all, I write in pencil

which requires more downward pressure than pen

erasing, continually erasing—rapidly back and forth

very similar motion and rpm's to you know what.

Triceps, biceps, rhomboids, trapezius

all screaming for relief in the name of artistically questionable
self-expression.

So when it comes time to throw the high hard one, as it were,

Mighty Casey at the bat, I guess you might say,

I summon in the left-handed relief pitcher

just up from triple A—very enthusiastically he sprints in from the bullpen

he's a little wild, a little raw…not much control yet, needs a bit of seasoning,

it's rumored he might even throw a spitball.

Do more of you want to leave? Please, don't worry, I probably would too.

But so here's the picture—TMI indeed.

Three in the afternoon, shades temporarily drawn

(I think the mailman saw me once, so I'm rather scrupulous about this)

Dockers loosely shackled about the ankles, Nikes likely still laced on,

crusty clean-up rag at the ready in the night-stand drawer

(a purist, I employ no pornography or lubrication)

cat curled up on the lower right corner of the bed

knowing by now to remain a safe distance away until it's all mercifully done with,

but bemusedly watching all the same,

just to make things even more self-consciously difficult.

Shoot a basketball with your left hand sometime, throw a Frisbee,

Hell, just try brushing your teeth.

In this ungainly manner I arhythmically toil—

ostensibly in the name of priapic pleasure.

Yet there's nothing to be ashamed of here—

it somehow seems so sordid, but why?

I mean, we all do it, it's perfectly natural.

Just ask Masters and Johnson, Dr. Ruth, Pee-wee Herman…

But for a sadly non-ambidextrous, hormonally bereft, libidinally challenged 52-year old,

the whole thing really is akin to savagely asphyxiating a cleverly evasive nautical invertebrate.

It just is.

Nothing cooperates.

In my mind's eye, I see my gloatingly remarried ex-wife, just laughing uproariously.

The phone rings—my mother leaves a rambling message about Thanksgiving.

Why? It's September.

A pair of those ill-dressed elderly religious women knock,

remain there peering curiously in, knock again.

And so the accordion discordantly collapses,

the dying balloon wrinkles helplessly to the floor.

A weary sigh. A pause to regroup.

It's never easy. This I stoically accept.

The cat, thinking it's finally over,

reaches extravagantly forward and stretches luxuriantly, as they do…

"No! No! Go back! Go back!" I shout—he quizzically retreats.

My fear is that he might ferally pounce

upon this helplessly writhing newborn marsupial.

Some lightning-quick Siegfried and Roy phallic mauling.

Try explaining that to the urgent care receptionist.

But I'm a plugger—so I grimly resume the joyless battering.

It's all mental now—you know how it is—

one trolls for just the appropriate electrifyingly illicit scenario.

Yes, there's a strap-on involved, verbal abuse, a voyeuristic third party, spanking.

God, I love the spanking.

I wish it weren't so…but desperate times call for…

Oh, how dreadful it all is, how unseemly—

Suddenly it's over. The cucumber is dead.

My delicate right arm duly preserved.

So with it,

I write you this.

WHAT HAPPENED?

It's hard enough, really

on a Tuesday afternoon

cracking like Humpty-Dumpty

splattering all over the clichéd couch

your soon to be ex-wife

solicitously stroking your repentant, heaving shoulders

she and the self-satisfied therapist

(how she found him, I'll never know)

exchanging heartfelt, patronizing glances

tut, tut, tut—oh, the ill-concealed smugness of it all!

Your testicles shrinking like time-lapse raisins

with each stultifying sob

pouring out your emasculated heart

a future of crappy apartments, redundant sandwiches,

and three-for-the-price-of-two, pre-owned porn

dead ahead

when, as you reach for the condescending Kleenex

the coup de grace, as it were;

the two-ply, extra-absorbent, filmy

flag of surrender

he so professionally proffers

you'd notice—out of the corner

of your swollen bloodshot eye

suddenly, yet unmistakably—could it really be?

He's grabbing a flashing, greedy, no doubt eyeful

of your woman's stupendous, traffic-stopping mammaries

at one hundred fifty overpriced dollars an hour.

No wonder he always took her side.

It wasn't this way with Dr. Shapiro, no

the sixtyish menschy Jew

a kindly kosher uncle if you will

pictures of his well-adjusted wife and children everywhere

the Parthenon, river-rafting, graduation ceremonies

little Shapiros whose tuitions my neuroses had largely paid.

Ditto Dr. Sidman years prior—

both professionally immune

to the sirenic lure

of a scantily clad softly sniffling shiksa's beguiling bosom.

No. She wanted a fresh, unbiased start.

Fresh, indeed—a six-foot-four

gold-chain wearing, Marlboro puffing

sports car driving, newly divorced

ex-Catholic school hoops star

real estate broker turned therapist

back issues of *GQ*, *Road and Track*, *Men's Health*

littering the waiting room coffee table

nary a *New Yorker* or *Atlantic* in sight

Oy Gevalt!

I don't blame the guy for looking

not since Tuesday had somehow become

Jayne Mansfield dress-up day

a nearly six-foot gleaming blonde glamazon

equal measure bodacious bombshell pin-up

unicorn straddling warrior princess

a sheerly plunging wonder-blouse

unabashedly, no, proudly pushing forth

those pendulous pillowy ellipses

straining like fecund cycloptic beasts

barely restrained by her besieged brassiere

a restless, clingy, upwardly mobile skirt—

her delectably hypnotic haunches

subtly shifting as she gravely, gracefully

uncrossed her endless, exquisite, exfoliated gams

leaned forward earnestly, provocatively, quite reasonably

articulated a litany of unmet needs

emotional and otherwise

one highly effective lonesome tear

bravely rappelling from those

too true baby blues.
How could he resist?

You know, for five or six years there
those breasts and everything attached to them
gave me life, nourished me
lent new and validating purpose
to matters both quotidian and existential.
I suppose it was a necessary visit
to a domestic reality
I had yet to experience
and never will again—
a normalcy I had always wondered about,
possibly craved, I didn't know.
Alas, it wasn't for me.
Like everywhere I've ever been,
a nice place to visit
but I wouldn't want
to live there.

OLD SCHOOL TIMMY

Hi my name's Timmy Archibald and I'm seven

going on eight and you're invited to my

birthday party at Magic Lane Fun Center

this Saturday but leave your sissy parents

at home 'cause we're bowling without those wimpy

little fences that block off the gutters so your

sensitive feelings won't get hurt because

you're too uncoordinated to roll a sparkly

eight-pound ball straight down the alley.

I'd rather bowl an honest seven than some pretend

sixty-three and if you cry for any

reason I'll sock your shoulder so hard

you'll really have something to cry about.

We're eating corn dogs and drinking Mountain Dew

and we're putting seventy-five cents in

the condom machine in the men's room even

if we have to stand on the garbage can

to do it let me tell you, show and

tell is gonna really be something on Monday.

If you're a spaz I'm not picking you for my team at recess.

Go play four square with the girls

or tetherball by yourself, creep.
I don't want fairy tales without kids
getting eaten I don't want a trophy
for picking my nose in right field
I'm sure as hell not hitting a baseball
off a tee and if you crowd the plate
I'll drill you just like my dad told me.
I can't stand grownups who wear costumes
on Halloween and take pictures of every dumb thing
their rotten kids do. I can cross the street
by myself so don't hold my hand I'm
almost eight for God's sakes.

My uncle told me back in the day
playgrounds had metal slides ten feet high
you could jump off and kids threw
dirt clods at each other real hard and
dogs would have fights like savage wild
animals and you could watch them have sex
and sometimes they'd end up stuck together
and you could ride in the open bed of a truck
or at least pack nine or ten kids in
a car all crazy like clowns at the circus.

Johnny's mom is a piece of ass, that's what
my dad says, I'm not sure what he means
but the other moms don't like her at all she
bartends at TGI Fridays where the
dads go to watch sports my mom works
at the daycare she hates my dad she
says he's emotionally bankrupt he works
at the lumber yard but his back hurts a lot.
He can't really play too much anymore.
He mostly just watches TV.
He was a great bowler before I was born,
he has trophies and a smashed-up old pin
with 300 written on it and pictures of him
smiling with other guys all wearing shiny shirts
that say Al's Refrigeration on them
they look really happy.
He's pretty fat now
and has to take pills for his heart
he has a girlfriend she's a hairdresser but
she usually comes over after I'm in bed
I hear them laughing then it's quiet.
Once I heard him tell her I was a mistake.
Mom says she's through with men the assistant
principal took her out a couple times she

says he's a goddam toe-licking pervert.

Mom and Dad went to counseling before they split

and the time I went I drew

pictures of how I felt.

Mostly they were of people

living deep underground.

I remember Mom cried real hard.

Dad just sat there, looking at his hands...

sometimes I wish I was invisible,

and no one would ever know I was there,

but I'd be there,

just kind of floating around, you know,

like a really nice ghost, or maybe just part of the air.

Pretty crazy, huh?

Anyway, the party's at three,

no grownups allowed.

ON PUBLISHING YOUR FRIEND

BY STEVE KETTMANN

This is what I wrote and published soon after Pete McLaughlin took his own life in Santa Cruz, California, in April 2017: I thought I had some understanding of the pain my friend Pete the Poet went through every week, probably every day, but I'm learning now how little I really understood. I know he struggled with a sense of feeling cut off from the world of other people, alienated and distanced, and the painful news that local poet Peter McLaughlin died on April 18 at age fifty-four, having taken his own life, has left me reeling with a sense of being alienated and distanced, as well. I've taken a baby step toward Pete's world, a world that I enter constantly through the words he left behind, a book of poems that I as his publisher had looked forward to bringing out until an anguished Pete told me no, he just couldn't handle that.

But Pete got too many things too right for me not to be haunted by the lines of his poems, the music of his pain, told with such clarity and humanity, courage and comic flair, that we laughed along with him and only rarely paused to tune into what lay under the surface. Pete, who grew up in San Francisco and moved to Santa Cruz in 2002, found a local following with regular appearances at open mics like the ones at the Ugly Mug and Santa Cruz Mountain Brewing. He showed up one Tuesday night here in Soquel for our regular open readings at the Wellstone Center in the Redwoods, the writers' retreat center I co-founded with my wife, Sarah, and I had no idea what to make of him. Sarah had heard Pete talking about his poetry that afternoon at the Buttery, and encouraged him to stop by.

I worried about what this innocuous-looking character might share under the label "poetry," with his wiry salt-and-pepper brush cut, the athletic thin build of a former runner and P.E. coach, and an open, engaging look that expressed both a low-simmering bewilderment with the world and a readiness to wink and turn that bewilderment into a joke. I braced myself for haikus on kitchen appliances or odes to the pitching style of Giants left-hander Madison Bumgarner.

Pete, bouncy with nervousness, told me he had written a poem called "I Wish I Was Billy Collins," a uniquely Pete mashup of gentle mockery and honest homage, and had actually put the poem in an envelope and mailed it off to the bestselling poet himself. Billy—outdoorsy poster boy of the *New Yorker*-and-NPR set—had written Pete back. And he'd sent a funny, implicitly approving note! Which as a matter of fact, Pete could pull out and read aloud right then and there for us! It was all pretty amazing, and Pete enjoyed winning the "Show and Tell" competition with such aplomb.

Pete read the poem aloud to us that first night, and looked jolted by the loud round of applause he received, as if his hair was standing on end. He raised his eyebrows and thanked us for listening, as he did so many times. He'd made us laugh, he'd made us smile wonderingly at all he'd packed into the lines, as he would again and again. Pete could describe the indescribable in a matter of fact way that, depending on the subject matter, was often hilarious, sometimes just random. He had periods where he visited every week to read his poems and periods where he stayed away, because he just couldn't grapple with the emotional roller coaster of feeling high over the way we all loved his poems and then being up all night, vibrating with self-doubt and self-loathing. During one of the periods where he was letting himself enjoy being embraced by us, he helped out with some chores before an event at the Wellstone Center and explained to me in meticulous detail that he was better at sweeping than anyone you'd ever meet, and demonstrated his technique, which was indeed remarkably efficient. Pete felt at home talking about sports, and when I told him what it was like hanging out with Dusty Baker or Bruce Bochy, a break from his episodic ambivalence about life seemed to come over him. We worked for months preparing his book, and Pete and our Wellstone Books intern Kyle would sit together for two or three hours at a time, going over line breaks and occasionally word choice, but mostly just getting silly and laughing so hard they cried.

I've always thought of breakthroughs in writing as offering a kind of handrail to take us deeper into life, but for Pete it wasn't like that. I didn't offer to publish him because it would be good for him, I offered to publish him because the world needed to see his stuff. When I talked to Casey Coonerty Protti, the owner of Book-shop Santa Cruz, about this remarkable unlikely talent, or to Eric at PGW, our distributor, I always had a cautious excitement, because with Pete you never knew. He used to show up at Bookshop and stand there imagining he was giving a reading, the focus of 40 sets of adoring eyes, and told me that after much practice he was ready for that. Then he changed his mind. Pete's poems worked best when he read them himself, the music of his pain coming alive with a kind of low key jazz beat, the exasperation underneath the words ebbing and flowing and sometimes exploding into a full-fledged rant, but above all a chord of hope or optimism sounding somewhere in the lines. He identifies so totally with an electric car in "Angry Prius" that it's both hilarious and exhilarating to hear him riff.

Pete would fold back into himself after he finished "Angry Prius," eyes down, his apologetic demeanor both comical and revealing. The poems were a way to share some small inkling of what it was like to be him, to have an imagination that rocketed through all the same private thoughts we have, just like us, but with more zany energy and freakishly spot-on detail than the rest of us can muster. Hearing him read, there was always astonishment in the air, the astonishment of seeing major talent face to face, and in so unlikely-seeming an individual, an unassuming divorced fiftysomething man living a quiet life in Santa Cruz. Pete understood all this—that, in fact, was part of the joke—and he had a way of reading where you could see him taken over by something beyond himself, something larger, that pulled him through the words, something that opened up to reveal what most of us keep hidden. Selfishly, we loved listening to him, even wondering what exactly it cost him to share so much. I never pushed Pete, except nudging him to read a favorite line one more time, when I knew he was up for it anyway. I didn't push him because I knew there was much I would not know and could not know about the private terrain of his dread.

Pete had his quirks, which he invited us to laugh about along with him. He had never owned a computer, and knew he never would. He talked of one day buying a cell phone, but the plan seemed farfetched. He wrote his poems out by hand in pencil and kept them in a binder, which he had a way of clutching in his lap, just before cracking it open to pick a poem to read, as if he feared it might explode in his lap. He'd gone so far as to duct-tape his binder shut one time and hide it away in his closet, half-convincing himself that it was gone; eventually he came around and cut it open again.

Now that he is gone, I feel myself flayed by the pain of losing him, disoriented by the suffocating weight of knowing I'll never talk to him again, never share a laugh. But with each day since I got the news, I'm trying to focus as well on the wonder of being friends with him, the wonder of sharing his moments of joy and happiness. He was arriving at the end of a long and harrowing journey each time he made it to easy-going and laughing, letting fly with another spontaneous hilarious line. I was lucky to share that with him. We were all lucky.

More than any other poem, I find myself going back to "Old School Timmy," a poem in a different key than most everything Pete wrote. He only read it aloud to us after much coaxing, underselling it in the extreme, but it was a revelation in its own way, autobiographical in a different way than most of his other work. Pete would fight back tears late in the poem as he read, but then look up smiling once he'd made it through another reading. He was still there. We were all still there.

SCHRÖDINGER'S HIPSTER

By Wallace Baine

The first time I heard Pete McLaughlin read his poems aloud—before he had even made it through the first one, in fact—I thought of Nabokov. God, that sounds so grandiose. Usually, when I hear poets that I don't know read their stuff, I think of baseball, though I try not to. It's just where my mind comes to rest at the first faint breeze of boredom. But Pete's writing really did make me think of Nabokov.

At the time, I had recently returned to *Lolita*, as I do periodically, to re-experience the thrill of a very specific kind of wit—remorseless, acidic, casually snotty, too anguished to be dishonest. These days, it's not advisable to regard Humbert Humbert with anything short of showy repugnance, at least for public consumption. But I have never been able to shake off the delight of diving into Humbert's distinct brand of self-loathing, the soul of erudition and refinement fighting every minute with the coarse, hairy-fisted, heavy-breathing beast with whom he has to share his mind and body. Whatever sense of theatrical but punishing self-negation that Nabokov could summon—whatever that thing is—Pete also had it. I told him so too. Though I wish I could have done so more elegantly.

When someone you know takes his own life, your mind starts racing. You can't help but replay a conversation here, an encounter there. And it's clear to me now that, in that moment in the reader's circle, I was too bubbly in my praise, too flip in my reaction. I nattered on about how the heart of comedy is in self-criticism, or some other movie-critic banality.

In truth, I was gobsmacked. In Pete's work, there is a kind of tensile-strength emotional honesty, the effect of which is like alpine lake water on your nut sack. What I said to him that night was simply a product of the shock of finding myself waist deep in Lake Tahoe in November. Sure, I was laughing, but it was involuntary, almost maniacal laughter. Wait, is he really talking about middle-aged male masturbation? That still tenacious taboo in a pan-sexual culture that celebrates every other imaginable kink? The last sexual horror, the most dependable metaphor for infinite sadness? Did he really liken it to "flogging a recalcitrant sway-backed donkey up a hill"? Of course, I fuckin' laughed. It was either that or peel my skin off with a sushi knife in shame and disgust.

Pete absorbed the hosannas around the room with the expression of a man suddenly struggling with a spastic colon. It was not a process he enjoyed. Writers, comedians, artists, all of us who face evaluation from other people—even something as friendly as Tuesday night OpenMic open reading at the Wellstone Center in the Redwoods—learn to build a psychic wall separating the "material" from our true selves. I'm not sure Pete was able to build such a wall. He only told me later that praise made him feel like a fraud.

And here I was, just about dancing on the table in enthusiasm for his work, which I hesitate to call "poetry," given my own biases against the prettified self so many poets labor to present to the world. Pete's stuff is not like that. It's ugly and sad and banal and outrageous. It's, in his own words, like "jagged kidney stones" that have to be passed with intense pain, but precious little relief.

Pete had a way of performing his poems that defied description. Words poured out of him with no artifice. He jabbed at them like he hated them. He spit them out and they landed with a plop at our feet. But he took no apparent delight in the spitting. Then I—boorishly, idiotically, like it was all one giant joke—suggested in all earnestness that he belonged on tour, that he could brilliantly establish a new kind of performance art form somewhere between stand-up comedy and the silly gimmickry of slam poetry. He could have pushed Billy Collins and Calvin Trillin into old-man irrelevance. The urbane clubsters burned out on Lewis Black angst but thirsting for authenticity would have loved him. Dude could have been a star.

But that wasn't Pete's game. He took seriously the truism that art is supposed to speak the truth, even when that truth cannot be separated from a toxic dose of self-hatred, even when telling that truth is an act of lacerating your own flesh. Sure, he'd bleed for you. But, applause? You want an encore? What, are you a sadist?

We became friends after that, Pete and I. We gingerly built our relationship upon the scaffolding of a kind of rarefied bro-speak, a realm of quasi-worship built on sports, politics, movies and music, the native language of graying hyper-literate liberal white males enjoying the perverse pageantry of American culture from the bleacher seats, but still all too aware of the traps and taboos that keep them well-behaved.

We dutifully touched upon the stations of the cross—Ali, *Apocalypse Now*, Bill Hicks, Rickey Henderson, Los Lobos, whatever we could find in the bag of permissible icons of durable cool that's not too hackneyed (cough ... The Clash ... cough). We tolerated each other's endorsements for this book or that movie, signaled our sophisticated and highly curated maleness through preference of adult beverage, and finally settled into a tentative joint exploration of our mutually tortured attitudes toward sex, money, family, aging, work and our respective places in the chimp hierarchy that obliges you to walk the high wire between public status and private self-respect.

Only occasionally would I venture onto the subject of his writing, never to nudge him to publish or to inflame his guilt for not publishing, but only to get him to talk about the circumstances of each piece.

He was clearly ambivalent about unleashing his work into the world, bound by the cold fear that someone somewhere somehow would call him on some contradiction or catch him in a lie, whether it was factual or emotional. Telling the truth is therapeutic if you're screaming it into the void. It only has consequences if someone hears it.

Laughing at Pete's writing in the wake of his death felt like cheap tragedy. But now, laughing at his words—"Bristling rogue hairs/somehow misplaced from a Turkish blacksmith/charge out insolently from my astonished nostrils"—is the most sincere tribute I can give him. His voice still rises from the page when I read his work now. It's a wonderful experience of literary synesthesia, and it's particularly vivid when he returns to the wretchedness of his living situation, the inventory of depressingly recurrent themes he had to wake up to every morning—the yellowing teeth, the puking cat, the various indignities of being a faceless drone in the aggressively nihilist consumer culture that we all must negotiate. The target of his broken-glass sense of humor was usually himself. In these poems, you find a species of self-loathing that spreads beyond his little studio apartment into the larger community from which he sprang.

Santa Cruz is not just an address. It is a specific brand of freak-flag lefty culture that is easily stereotyped but not so easy to fully comprehend unless you swim in it daily, as Pete did. Sure, he'd be more than happy to disembowel himself as an "archetypal bitterly confused mateless misanthrope," but he was going to take Santa Cruz down with him. "I'd rather get dengue fever," he wrote, "and be discovered dead with giant African maggots feasting on my eyeballs than find myself taking a freaking selfie at Burning Man." Such talk in Santa Cruz can sound like heresy.

Pete simply could not abide what he saw as the phony, smug, self-absorbed, Whole-Foodsier-than-thou, namaste culture that defines Santa Cruz and places like it. Kale, Jack Johnson, the Toyota Prius, Noam Chomsky, saying "No worries" instead of "You're welcome"—it was all a parade of horrors for him. His critiques of Santa Cruz certainly drew blood, but he was no right-wing incel tub-thumper (however much "The Woman of My Dreams" plays with that fantasy). He was—fundamentally, inescapably—one of us, simultaneously perfectly comfortable and painfully uncomfortable reading poetry and sipping coffee in a snooty café. He was Schrödinger's hipster.

Where is the place in today's call-out culture for a person whose ambivalence goes up to 11? For someone who has so deeply internalized the indictment against the straight white male but still wakes up every morning in the skin of such a creature? The death in the summer of 2018 of celebrity chef Anthony Bourdain, who had times seemed like the most self-actualized person on the planet, brought into the mainstream the radical notion that suicide is sometimes not (maybe never) a function of bad life circumstances.

These days, the most pressing spiritual question that every reflective, even moderately self-aware person must daily ask him or herself is—to put it in contemporary vernacular—"Am I an asshole?" And honesty demands from everyone short of Mister Rogers (and, I suspect, even him too) to at least answer "Sometimes" or "A little bit." Pete's poetry exposes his inner assholery—at least as it's measured in a culture of self-affirmation and pep talks to the mirror—in the same way that Humbert Humbert exposed Nabokov's inner depravity.

Pete was a really good guy, funny, sweet-natured, compassionate, a great listener. Maybe he was just unequipped to live with the duality between his persona on the page and his "real" self in the produce section at Shopper's Corner. Maybe he saw that separation as more an uncrossable chasm than it really was. Maybe a swan dive into that chasm was the only gesture that, in the end, really made any sense.

About Wellstone Books

Wellstone Books is the publishing arm of the Wellstone Center in the Redwoods — **www.wellstoneredwoods.org** – a small writers' retreat center in Northern California founded in 2012 by Sarah Ringler and Steve Kettmann. WCR offers writing residencies, fellowships and three-month resident internships for aspiring writers, and hosts periodic Author Talk events with writers like Mary Roach, Cara Black, Jonathan Franzen and Viet Thanh Nguyen. Wellstone Books does not accept unsolicited manuscripts, but we are always looking for writers who are familiar with our publishing philosophy and want to work with us to develop future projects. Interested writers, or journalists in search of review copies or author availability, write to: **steve@wellstoneredwoods.org**.

Also Available From Wellstone Books

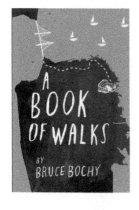

A Book of Walks
BY BRUCE BOCHY

The manager of the San Francisco Giants, having taken his team to World Series victories in 2010, 2012 and 2014, is known nationally for his rare knack for staying on an even keel even in the midst of some very stressful situations. How does he do it? One thing he's always tried to do is get in regular long walks, which help him clear his head and get over the disappointments of the day. This pocket-sized volume, dubbed "an endearing little book" by the *New York Times*, takes us with Bochy on eight talks around the country, each its own chapter (complete with map of his route). Come along for the ride on walks through Central Park in New York, along Lake Michigan in Chicago and across San Francisco to the Golden Gate Bridge. How does Bochy keep a cool head, the Toronto *Globe and Mail* asked?

"In the tradition of thinkers like Rousseau, Kant and Thoreau, Bochy, sixty, swears by long strolls and vigorous walks — 'the freedom to be alone with my thoughts for a while' — which he makes time for wherever he is," Nathalie Atkinson writes.

A Book of Walks, a Northern California bestseller, makes a memorable gift for any baseball fan — or fan of walks.

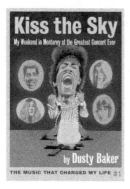

Kiss the Sky: My Weekend in Monterey at the Greatest Concert Ever
By Dusty Baker

For his eighteenth birthday, Dusty Baker's mother gave him a great present: Two tickets to the Monterey Pop Festival of June 1967, a three-day event featuring more than thirty bands, and use of the family station wagon for the weekend so young Dusty could drive down from Sacramento to the Monterey Bay. He was another young person, trying to take it all in, sleeping on the beach with his buddy, having the time of his life soaking up the vibe and every different musical style represented there. Baker's lifelong love of music was set in motion, his wide-ranging, eclectic tastes, everything from country to hip-hop. He also caught the Jimi Hendrix Experience, who put on such a show that to this day Baker calls Hendrix the most exciting performer he's ever seen. He went on to years of friendship with musicians from B.B. King and John Lee Hooker to Elvin Bishop. This account grabs a reader from page one and never lets up.

"At its best, the book evokes not only the pleasure of music, but the connection between that experience and the joy of sports," *NewYorker.com* writes.

"Reading *Kiss the Sky* is like having a deep conversation with Dusty Baker – about baseball, fathers and sons, race, culture, family, religion, politics – and always music," says Joan Walsh of MSNBC. "He doesn't sugarcoat anything, but he makes you feel good about being alive nonetheless."

#1 in Wellstone Books' "Music That Changed My Life" series.

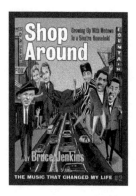

Shop Around: Growing Up With Motown in a Sinatra Household
BY BRUCE JENKINS

Bruce Jenkins was twelve years old, living in Malibu with his parents, when he heard the original "Shop Around" single, by "The Miracles featuring Bill 'Smokey' Robinson," the first Billboard No. 1 R&B single for Motown's Tamla label. Released nationally in October 1960, the single would ultimately make it into the Grammy Hall of Fame, and for young Bruce, it was a revelation. Jenkins grew up surrounded by music. His father, Gordon Jenkins, was a composer and arranger who worked with artists from Ella Fitzgerald and Billie Holiday to Louis Armstrong and Johnny Cash, but was best known for his close collaboration with Frank Sinatra. His mother, Beverly, was a singer. For Bruce, "Shop Around" ushered him into a new world of loving Motown. In *Shop Around*, he brings to life the first thrill of having the music claim him, sketches from his life with his father and mother, and traces how his love of music has grown and evolved over the years.

"Bruce Jenkins manages to accomplish the always dangerous task of describing music with words as well as anyone I've read," rocker Huey Lewis says. "His knowledge is formidable and his passion is infectious."

"A warm and witty memoir about how music binds us all," according to Joel Selvin, *San Francisco Chronicle* pop music critic.

"An absolutely essential read. An awesome story about a priceless time in music history," adds Emilio Castillo, Bandleader for Tower of Power.

#2 in Wellstone Books' "Music That Changed My Life" series.

Night Running: A Book of Essays About Breaking Through

This daring volume combines the best of writing on running with the appeal of the best literary writing, essays that take in the sights and sounds and smells of real life, of real risk, of real pain and of real elation. Emphasizing female voices, this collection of eleven personal essays set in different countries around the world offers a deep but accessible look at the power of running in our lives to make us feel more and to see ourselves in a new light.

From acclaimed novelist Emily Mitchell and Portland writers Anne Milligan and Pete Danko and authors Vanessa Runs and Steve Kettmann to Bonnie Ford, T.J. Quinn and Joy Russo-Schoenfield of ESPN, a diverse lineup of writers captures a variety of perspectives on running at night. These are stories that can inspire people of all ages and backgrounds to take on a thrilling new challenge. The contributors all have distinct tales to tell, but each brings a freshness and depth to their experiences that make *Night Running* a necessary part of every runner's library - and a valuable addition to the reading lists of all thoughtful readers. We're putting together a Night Running 2 collection; writers interested in contributing should email us at info@well-stoneredwoods.org for guidelines.

"A book for anyone who has used solitude and exertion to explore a new crevice of their own mind. Fear, exhilaration, anger, accomplishment, despair, euphoria — every one of these emotions is distilled in *Night Running*."
— David Epstein, *The Sports Gene*

"A fascinating and eclectic collection! In Night Running, eleven essayists express, with bracing honesty, how a simple act of will—running in the dark—can free body and mind from fear, and restore the spirit."
— Novelist Mary Volmer, author of *Crown of Dust* and *Reliance, Illinois*

"*Night Running* captures in a myriad of ways the essence of running: solitude, self-discovery and the exhilaration of a momentary escape from the banal."
— Sandy Alderson, general manager, New York Mets, 2:53 marathoner

CPSIA information can be obtained
at www.ICGtesting.com
Printed in the USA
BVHW031548091220
595287BV00001B/1

9 780960 061556